Jossey-Bass Teacher

Jossey-Bass Teacher provides K–12 teachers with essential knowledge and tools to create a positive and lifelong impact on student learning. Trusted and experienced educational mentors offer practical classroom-tested and theory-based teaching resources for improving teaching practice in a broad range of grade levels and subject areas. From one educator to another, we want to be your first source to make every day your best day in teaching. *Jossey-Bass Teacher* resources serve two types of informational needs—essential knowledge and essential tools.

Essential knowledge resources provide the foundation, strategies, and methods from which teachers may design curriculum and instruction to challenge and excite their students. Connecting theory to practice, essential knowledge books rely on a solid research base and time-tested methods, offering the best ideas and guidance from many of the most experienced and well-respected experts in the field.

Essential tools save teachers time and effort by offering proven, ready-to-use materials for in-class use. Our publications include activities, assessments, exercises, instruments, games, ready reference, and more. They enhance an entire course of study, a weekly lesson, or a daily plan. These essential tools provide insightful, practical, and comprehensive materials on topics that matter most to K–12 teachers.

"We particularly like the *Phonics Pathways* program. For the average—and certainly the new—homeschooling parent, I enjoy the simplicity, yet completeness, *of Phonics Pathways*. Everything you need is included in the book. Instructions are concise, clear, and free of professional vocabulary. It's one of our favorite books!"

—Jessie Wise and Susan Wise Bauer
The Well-Trained Mind: A Guide to Classical Education At Home

"Within seven weeks, all thirty-two first graders in my classroom of various ability levels became readers. Explicit phonics and blending instruction are the keys to this success. In addition, it is vital for students to have sufficient practice with decodable text to cement the rules and skills already learned.

"Dorbooks' *Phonics Pathways* and *Pyramid* have helped my students tremendously! The phonics rules included in *Phonics Pathways* empower my students to drive through words with ease. *Pyramid* has been especially fabulous for the slower students who sometimes reverse letters—reversals have diminished considerably. Now they are diving into marvelous literature with confidence and pride. In March we had a literature evening for parents, and all of my students took turns reading selections from *The Book of Virtues!*"

—Pamela M. Barret, First-Grade Teacher
Tovashal Elementary School, Murrieta, CA
NRRF "Teacher of the Year" 1998

"Our two adopted seven-year-old sons are learning disabled, and one of them has ADD as well. He is repeating his SLD second grade class. After only two months of *Phonics Pathways* he is reading at the upper level of grade three—it is a miracle!

"My son's speech pathologist is now using it with her fourteen-year-old student, and three other teachers are waiting to get their copy. The wealth of word lists, spelling rules, blending exercises, and practice sentences make it a rich resource that would enhance any reading program.

"When I finally had to return my library copy the woman standing in back of me put it on reserve for herself. If everyone knew how easy and fast this book works and how inexpensive it is, it would put the more expensive programs right out of business."

—Bonnie Miller, Mom
Greenacres, Florida

"Our elementary instructors are inserviced in the use of *Phonics Pathways*. They have experienced great success in using it with a wide variety of students: English as a Second Language, remedial, beginning reading, dyslexic, and even adults.

"It is clear and well organized, and has large print. The skills are sequenced correctly, the sketches humorous, the proverbs encouraging, and the hints very useful. Combining reading and spelling and applying the skill in words and sentences is most helpful.

"This outstanding resource has helped many students learn to read and spell, and given teachers confidence in teaching phonics, spelling, and reading. I highly recommend it for all students who are learning to read."

—Christine Knight, Faculty Facilitator
Schoolcraft College, Michigan

"I am a special ed teacher at a day treatment program. These are the kids no school knows how to handle anymore but are not severe enough to go into a residential program. Half my kids have severe learning problems leading to behavior problems, and half have severe behavior problems leading to learning problems.

I tried *Phonics Pathways*, and the results are really good! My 4th and 5th graders who read at a kindergarten level before we started now can read many words after only 18 lessons. The blending exercises taught them how to decode words, and they now automatically use the same strategies to decode new and long words.

The parents of these kids think I am some kind of genius because finally I got their kids to read. And it's so beautiful and rewarding to see their self esteem grow also—this is what makes teaching so rewarding. Thank you *sooo* much for your book!

—Renee Wesly, Special Ed Teacher
Maunawili Elementary School
Kailua, Hawai

"I started *Phonics Pathways* in K3, the last year of kindergarten in Taiwan. After only four months these six- and seven-year-olds began reading story books and never looked back! K3 has surpassed my wildest dreams, as they read far better than any other class at school. They put students who've studied for up to six years to shame.

"One mother told me her daughter reads her e-mail, and although it has a lot of technical terms her daughter reads it better than she does. And she has a college degree! Parents are amazed that their little ones can read at such an early age, even before they are quite at ease with Chinese characters.

"A funny story: I was substitute teaching an older class that had been learning English for at least six years. When I told them K3 could read better and more fluent than they could they laughed and didn't believe me. Just then, Sunny, a K3 student passed, and I called her in. We held a reading contest, and little Sunny beat the whole class!"

—Rudi Kerkhoffs
Kindergarten & First Grade Teacher
Taiwan

"Lowell School District has implemented Dorbooks' educational material with all the students in our Title I Program. This is a carefully researched, no-frills program with a simple format and easy implementation, requiring little or no preparation time. It fits into our existing reading program, and is flexible enough for individual or group work.

"Our teachers are experiencing great success with this material, and are very excited! Kindergarteners are exploring the sounds consonants make when followed by vowels. At midyear third graders' word study scores went up an average of 22 percentile points, and reading comprehension an average of 26 points.

"*Phonics Pathways* unlocks the secrets of sound-symbol relationships, allowing comprehension to become the focus. Students are now able to read words they could only guess at before, and have strategies to decode unknown words. They can focus on the real purpose of reading—*meaning*. Our teachers are thrilled!"

—Bettina Dunne, Reading Teacher
Lowell Joint School District
Whittier, CA

Phonics Pathways

Clear Steps to Easy Reading and Perfect Spelling, 9th Edition

Dolores G. Hiskes

JOSSEY-BASS
A Wiley Imprint
www.josseybass.com

Published by Jossey-Bass
A Wiley Imprint
989 Market Street, San Francisco, CA 94103-1741   www.josseybass.com

Jossey-Bass books and products are available through most bookstores. To contact Jossey-Bass directly call our Customer Care Department within the U.S. at 800-956-7739, outside the U.S. at 317-572-3986, or fax 317-572-4002.

Jossey-Bass also publishes its books in a variety of electronic formats. Some content that appears in print may not be available in electronic books.

ISBN: 0-7879-7910-4

Printed in the United States of America
FIRST EDITION
PB Printing   10 9 8 7 6

About this Book

With the use of a clever icon, Dewey the Bookworm, *Phonics Pathways* teaches phonics and spelling using an efficient, practical, and foolproof method. The comprehensive spelling rules were gathered from classic old reading and spelling texts in English-speaking countries all over the world.

Phonics Pathways is organized by sounds and spelling patterns. They are introduced one at a time, and slowly built into words, phrases, and sentences. Simple step-by-step directions begin every lesson. Extensive examples, word lists, and practice readings are 100 percent decodable.

• Each new step builds upon previously learned skills for continuous review and reinforcement. Learning in small, incremental steps is easier for everyone, especially students with learning disabilities or very short attention spans.

• A multisensory method is used to address all learning styles, and every letter introduced is illustrated with multiple pictures beginning with its sound. These features are especially helpful to second-language students.

• Reading and spelling are taught as an integrated unit. Research shows that accurate spelling is critical to the reading process (see "Spelling," *Phonics Pathways* 9th edition, page 262). Teaching reading and spelling together reinforces and enhances each skill.

• Extensive reproducible games, activities, and teaching aids make both teaching and learning fun and easy. Students achieve maximum results in the minimum time with the least amount of effort and expense.

Although most appropriate for K-2 emergent readers, this award-winning book also is successfully being used with adolescent and adult learners, as well as second language learners and students with learning disabilities.

Perfect for both schools and for use at home, this classic text offers specific strategies for dyslexic readers as well as beginners. Wise humorous proverbs encourage virtues such as patience, perseverance, honesty, kindness, compassion, courage, and loyalty.

The Author

Dolores G. Hiskes (Livermore, California) has tutored reading for over thirty years. She has collected classic old reading and spelling texts from English-speaking countries all over the world, which are incorporated into her instruction. She has implemented a number of school and community tutoring programs using her materials, such as the highly touted YES Reading Center in Palo Alto, CA. Well–published in professional journals and a winner of numerous honors, she also publishes a free on-line newsletter about teaching reading called *Phonics Talk* (www.dorbooks.com).

CONTENTS

ACKNOWLEDGMENTS

I am always and forever grateful to:
Our beloved children Robin and Grant who inspired a passion for
teaching reading in the very beginning...our sweet young grandchildren
Connor and Austen who have rekindled this passion...
Bob Sweet of the National Right to Read Foundation for his extraordinary support
and encouragement...Sherrill Fink for such eagle-eyed editing, proofreading,
and marvelous ideas (her husband also!)...Lindsay Pavel and Susan Ebbers for their
warm friendship and invaluable feedback...Bay Area Independent Publishers
Association for all the publishing help... my awesome wizard friends
Randy Alford, Pete Masterson, Jon Kalb, Keith Fox, and George Pavel
for their amazing tech support (it's all still magic to me!)...
my good friends Barbara and Norm of Rayve Productions and
Barbara of The Intrepid Group for such great fulfillment and sage advice...
May May Gong of Northwest Digital Designs for a stunning web site...
the talented and dedicated tutors at the YES reading program in Menlo Park
and Stanford University who have given so generously
of their time, talents, and resources to this extraordinary program...
Family, friends, and all the original authors from all over the world
(whoever they are and wherever they now might be, on or under the ground!)
for the marvelous collection of proverbs...
my eternal love and gratitude to my beloved best friend Johnny...
a shiny gold medal for his love, support, and invaluable (if blunt) critiques,
and a big purple heart for his valiant battles with insomnia
while pretending to sleep through the neverending 4:00 a.m. clicking, whirring,
and whining of the computer and laser printer in our bedroom.
Last but not least, a heartfelt and humble thanks to Steve Thompson
and the rest of the great crew at Jossey-Bass for sharing my vision.
This little book will reach far more people with them at the helm
and I am very grateful for that. I will still be here
to help you in any way that I can, as always.
Now it's time for Dewey and me to thank all of you
for letting this book be part of your lives.
It's been wonderful!
Love,

Dolores

"The pleasantest of all diversions

is to sit alone under a tree...

A book spread out

before you...

and to

make friends

with

people of a

distant past

you have

never

known."

—Adapted
from Kenko
1300 A.D.

POEMS

Phonics Pathways: Clear Steps to Easy Reading and Perfect Spelling

INTRODUCTION

READING is a conversation between a reader and an author. It is our "remote control" to faraway places and long-ago times. The poem on the previous page, for example, was written over six hundred years ago! If it were not for the written word, every time someone dies an entire library would die with him.

WHY PHONICS?

Everyone ought to know the joy of decoding an unfamiliar word, syllable by syllable, exploring the uncharted world of new words and fresh ideas. If we are limited to reading only words we know, and guessing at new words through context clues, we are confined within the boundaries of our current vocabularies and thoughts, interpreting things only from within our own shallow perspectives.

When children enter first grade, their comprehension vocabulary is estimated to be upward of 20,000 words. Phonics is the clearest connecting link between this vocabulary and the printed page. After learning these sound-to-symbol skills, most children are able to read almost anything their speaking and listening vocabularies and interests allow, unlimited by "readability formulas" or simplified in any other way. It gives students the key to read words they already know, and the skills to look up words they don't know, allowing comprehension to happen. They are able to read the words they could only guess at before, and can focus on the real purpose of reading—*meaning*.

With *direct* or *explicit* phonics the 44 sounds and 200 spelling patterns accounting for the great majority of words in the English language are learned first, one at a time, and gradually combined and recombined into words and sentences. Reading is taught like any other complex skill such as learning how to dance or play the piano. One note, step, or sound is learned at a time and very gradually combined into more complicated chords, routines, or syllables and words. Sight-reading whole groups of notes at a time, or combining steps into an entire dance routine, or reading whole sentences and books, is what occurs naturally as a *result* of training and practice, and should never be used as a teaching tool in the beginning. Phonics is the process—sight reading is the result.

DON'T CHILDREN HAVE DIFFERENT LEARNING MODES?

Children do have different learning modes. Therefore, we have presumed it necessary to tailor reading methods to perceptual styles. No research has ever validated this approach. Studies conclusively prove that letter knowledge and phonemic awareness are the best indicators of reading success. And if a multisensory approach is used to teach phonics, then all students will learn, whether auditory, visual, or kinesthetic. A multisensory method has the synergistic effect of addressing the strongest learning mode while reinforcing the weakest. *How* students learn is different—but *what* students learn should be the same. Everyone should be able to decode the longest of unfamiliar words, syllable by syllable, whatever their learning mode.

DON'T WE TEACH PHONICS NOW?

The most common reading programs today are based on *literature* or *whole language,* whereby students learn to read by being exposed to good classic literature. The premise is that being able to read is a *developmental* skill, as is being able to walk or talk. Words are first learned as a whole—the critical initial step of teaching letter sounds and blending them into syllables is not included. Spelling is not taught in systematic patterns, but taken from the story being read in a random fashion. What if we had to learn mathematics "times tables" randomly, such as 9 x 7, 12 x 8, 6 x 13? It would be most difficult, indeed!

If a student needs assistance with a word, "phonetic hints" are given by naming the beginning and ending letter sounds, but students must then guess to fill in the middle part. Students are also encouraged to guess at words through sentence context clues—story meaning is stressed over word accuracy. It is perfectly acceptable to substitute "house" for "home" because the meaning is the same. But as Mark Twain once wrote: "The difference between the right word and the almost right word is the difference between lightning and the lightning bug"!

Consider the words "laparoscopy" and "lobotomy." They each begin and end with the same letters. They each have a similar shape. They each have similar meanings (both are surgical procedures) when taken in general context. Few of us, however, would wish for a surgeon who was only able to read these words by shape, beginning and ending letters, and context clues! With explicit phonics these words are read by syllables: "lap-a-ros-co-py" or "lo-bot-o-my." There is no chance of ever confusing one with the other. There really is a world of difference between being *almost* right and *exactly* right!

Are mistakes like this really made? In Virginia a teacher was recently hired to tutor a licensed pharmacist who could not discern the difference between "chlorpropamide," which lowers blood sugar, and "chlorpromazine," which is an antipsychotic. Similar stories happen all too frequently.

When words are learned individually as wholes, each word is stored in its own "document" in the brain, making retrieval time-consuming and difficult. This frequently results in students reading slowly and laboriously, and never for pleasure. Progress can remain slow and uncertain. Sometimes the brighter the child the more difficulty he may have, since his logical mind can rebel unless he is able to connect it all into a framework that makes sense. Trying to teach young children how to read using only a whole-word method can result in highly-stressed fearful youngsters who feel they are failures when they are unable to read.

In summary, explicit phonics builds words from single letters, moving from the *smallest parts to the whole.* Implicit phonics teaches the whole word first, moving from the *whole to the smallest parts.* This difference is critical as they have vastly different results. Some reading programs claim to teach phonics with titles such as "Balanced Reading Program," "Systematic Contextual Phonics," "Embedded Phonics," "Phonemic Awareness," etc. These programs are *implicit phonics,* whereby words are still learned as wholes. Since the word "phonics" is so misunderstood, one must always look beyond the title into the reading program itself.

Why is there so much confusion if explicit phonics is so effective? Most likely it is because for over forty years we have been without not only phonics texts but also courses in teachers' colleges that include this kind of instruction. Most of the classic phonics reading and spelling textbooks have long been out of print.

Phonics Pathways: Clear Steps to Easy Reading and Perfect Spelling

Almost everyone would agree that "reading for meaning" should be a primary objective with *any* reading method. But how is this goal best achieved? When students are able to effortlessly decode their already considerable comprehension vocabulary, they are joyously freed to "read for meaning" instead of having to struggle while "meaning to read." They can focus on the *meaning* of what they are reading because the *mechanics* of sound-to-symbol relationships have already been learned and practiced until they are automatic.

The brain is not unlike a computer insofar as memory and retrieval are concerned. We might think of explicit phonics as a software program, the logical framework into which patterns and categories of words are organized and filed. Words can be quickly retrieved when reading, and skills do not fade. Learning to read by logical patterns results in clear, precise thinking, a skill which enhances everything children do. Math frequently improves as reading develops, and spelling improves dramatically!

WHAT ABOUT DYSLEXIA?

Dyslexia is a difficult problem, with no easy answers. The original definition described adults who had lost their ability to read following a stroke or injury. Its present usage is more generic, referring to reading disorders known or unknown, frequently resulting in word or letter confusion and/or reversal.

However, it has been my experience in thirty years of tutoring that many students who had been labeled dyslexic no longer reversed letters or words after having been taught explicit phonics. Many were no longer hyperactive. Behavior problems diminished or disappeared.

In medical references, dyslexia essentially is defined as "failure to see or hear similarities or differences in letters or words…tendency to substitute words for those he cannot see…" Guessing! Our students are trained to do the very thing that medical journals define as dyslexic.

A compelling hypothesis is that those students who no longer had dyslexic symptoms after having been taught explicit phonics were not really dyslexic to begin with, but only suffering from a lack in their educational training. Students cannot be expected to know what they may never have been taught, just as teachers cannot teach what they may not know.

Current research shows early reversals to be a normal developmental stage for many children. Just as crawling prepares a child for walking, incorporating blending skills when teaching beginning reading will help pattern eyes to move smoothly from left to right across the page, strengthening eye-tracking skills and preventing or correcting reversals. It is *essential* that students receive training in blending letters and syllables when first learning how to read, or to remediate established patterns of reversals!

Many students learn how to read easily and effortlessly after being taught letter sounds and blending skills. Those students who are truly dyslexic need more time and practice to develop fluent reading skills. The time it takes to acquire these skills varies greatly with each child, but the end result is ease and fluency of reading with excellent comprehension—a genuine and effortless enjoyment of all the wonderful stories in today's literature-rich curricula.

WHAT ABOUT INVENTED SPELLING?

The idea behind invented spelling is that students will remain free and creative, and "grow into" correct spelling later. But however we learn something the first time tends to "stick," even if it is wrong. For example, if we learn someone's name incorrectly it seems that we are forever calling them by that name. It takes some time and effort to correct. Recent research has also revealed that accurate spelling is critical to the reading process, and to whatever extent this knowledge is missing it is strongly associated with specific learning disability. Invented spelling is *not* true freedom!

IS PHONEMIC AWARENESS THE SAME THING AS PHONICS?

Phonemic awareness is the ability to hear sounds within a word when it is spoken. It is an *auditory* skill. Recent research has shown it to be the critical first step in learning how to read. Rhyming, singing, and reading aloud to children will help develop this skill. While phonemic awareness is an important *precursor to* phonics, it should never be confused with *instruction in* phonics, which is visual *and* auditory. For example, you could listen to the following word over and over again and thoroughly know the sounds in it. Now try reading it (in Russian!): РЭД How in the world would being phonemically aware of the *sounds* in this word ever be of any help whatsoever in actually *reading* it? Only by knowing the letter-sound relationships can this word ever be correctly read (turn upside down): ¡pǝɹ = p−ǝ−ᴚ ·p = Ⓨ ·ǝ = Ɛ ·ɹ = Ρ

WHEN SHOULD CHILDREN LEARN HOW TO READ?

Four to six-year olds can and should be taught letter sounds and blending skills in order to provide a solid foundation of reading basics. All children this age love to make noises, build things and take things apart. This is the proper age to teach the letters of the alphabet, the sounds they make, and beginning blending skills!

After that, some children will be able to blend sounds together faster than others. Others may be able to sound out a word rather quickly, but it may be months before they are able to read even short phrases. It may even take some students years to be able to read sentences. It is the ability to put these skills together which allows children to read books, and this varies greatly with each child. It is a developmental stage which depends upon how mature his nervous system is, and when his eyes are able to track smoothly from left to right across a page. One thing it has *nothing* to do with is intelligence, any more than wearing glasses does.

Once students have solid phonics skills under their belt they are ready to begin reading beginning readers. While it's true that schools implementing phonics and literature together do show positive results, it always takes longer to do it that way with a lot more work on the students' part. The more phonics skills students possess before reading "real" books, the stronger their reading will be. It is my experience that if a student waits to read books until they are able to read the *Pyramid* exercise on page 50, they will achieve maximum results in the minimum time with the least amount of effort. Students will then possess the gift of literacy at its most vital and fundamental level—the ability to read with ease, accuracy, fluency, and most of all...

... great enjoyment!

Note: Throughout this book the word "him" refers to male and female students equally.

GETTING STARTED

Find a time and place that is quiet and satisfactory for both of you. Go slowly, and genuinely praise his efforts. Be gently persistent in working every day—daily practice is essential!

However, do not hurry or pressure your student. There may even be times when it's best to put lessons aside for a while. Many things affect a child's receptiveness to learning, such as maturity, attention span, health, hyperactivity, etc. Attention span can vary greatly with each child, and even from day to day with the same child.

Read all of the directions in each lesson before you begin, and *always* do these lessons in sequence. This is important because one skill builds upon another, and each practice reading reflects knowledge of all the letter sounds learned up to that point.

At first, work only a few minutes a day. It is the *habit* of sitting together for a lesson that is important to establish—you will gradually find yourselves spending more time with these lessons. Success breeds confidence and enthusiasm on the student's part, and a desire to do more. However, lessons never need to be longer than 10 or 15 minutes to show real progress.

Keep studying one lesson until your child knows it thoroughly. The goal is not just to impart knowledge, but to make it *automatic* in recall. Reading these letter sounds should not be a conscious effort; it should be as effort-*less* and automatic as saying his own name. Your student should move ahead when he is completely ready—*never* according to "age or page." He might complete several pages in one day, or need many days to complete one page.

Following is a sample lesson plan for teaching the short-vowel sounds. It has proven to be an effective, seven-step strategy for many students, but can be modified or changed in any way:

1. Complete the first lesson on page one, following the step-by-step directions.

2. Play *Memory*. Find a box with a cover, and let him help you collect things to put into it, such as a pin, ball, eraser, sock, envelope, paper clip, etc. Have him choose one item, feel it, and put it in the box. Close the cover and ask him what is inside. Keep repeating this process, adding one item at a time, until he can no longer name the objects in the same order. This game develops his concentration, memory, and ability to recall images sequentially.

3. Re-read the lesson. Think of words that rhyme with this sound, including nonsense words.

4. Get a book of jokes or riddles, and tell him one—he will enjoy sharing it with his friends!

5. Play the *Short-Vowel Shuffle*. (See page 4. Also, make him a *Short-Vowel Stick* (page 3).

6. Read to him. There are excellent guides available suggesting wonderful books for every age level. Choose books for the beauty of the language, even though they will be beyond his current reading capability—after all, it is good music that inspires us, not piano drills!

7. Reward him:
    (a) Give him a coin to put in a special jar, but do not let him keep it until some agreed-upon time (end of year, birthday, etc.). He may only hold and count the coins at the end of the lesson, while you are reading to him. Remind him that each coin represents a lesson he has had, and that his "bank" of skills is growing along with his "bank" of money, or,
    (b) Give him a sticker to put on a 3" x 5" card. Let him keep the card when it is full and/or trade it in for a prize.

ABOUT PHONICS PATHWAYS

Phonics Pathways is organized by sounds and spelling patterns. They are introduced one at a time and slowly built into words, syllables, phrases, and sentences. Each new step builds upon previously learned skills for continuous review and reinforcement. Learning in small, incremental steps is easier for everyone, especially students with learning disabilities or very short attention spans. A multisensory method is used to address all learning styles.

Short-vowel sounds are presented first—they are the basic foundation that is needed to build good reading and spelling skills. They are best learned in isolation. In the beginning, many children are unable to hear these sounds *within* a word—accordingly, every letter introduced has multiple illustrations of objects *beginning* with its sound. Listening for and identifying these sounds develops phonemic awareness, which is the important first step in learning how to read. Multiple pictures more accurately illustrate the subtle range of sounds comprising each letter—similar in effect to that of a 3-D hologram.

These sounds and syllables are learned in the same way that we learn math—by pattern, and in order of complexity. Only the simplest and most regular spelling of each sound is presented at first. Spelling variations and sight words are not introduced until basic reading skills are well established. "Red," for example, is learned with other short "e" words on page 39, but "blue" is not introduced until page 165, with other "ue" vowel digraph words such as "true." This strategy makes learning and assimilation much easier, especially for bilingual students whose primary language may have only one sound per letter.

Graduated blending exercises are incorporated as part of the teaching technique in this book. These blending exercises ("eyerobics") begin with seventeen pages of two-letter blends to establish smooth, strong left-to-right eye tracking skills. Blending practice is critical to the reading process, and helps prevent or correct reversals. It also smooths out choppy reading, such as "kuh-a-t" for "cat."

Two-letter blends are integrated into meaningful words as soon as possible, beginning with three-letter words. They are not taught first as a separate set of disconnected skills to memorize before being applied. Memory experts have long known that it is much easier to remember something new if we are able to connect it to something else that is already known. Blending sounds into words we already know also helps prevent the "reading-without-understanding" syndrome sometimes seen when phonograms are learned in isolation.

Two-word phrases build into three-word sentences, etc.—gradually increasing in length and complexity. Many children have difficulty moving directly from words into whole sentences, and need this gradual transition. Eye span increases as eye tracking strengthens.

Reading and spelling are taught as an integrated unit—teaching them together reinforces and enhances each skill. Accuracy in reading and spelling is taught from the very first lesson.

Phonics Pathways contains all of the spelling rules and is a complete spelling reference. While it is not necessary to know all of these rules in order to read, this knowledge is a real shortcut to spelling accuracy. For example, some words are spelled "-able" and others "-ible," as in "appeasable, visible, taxable, edible"—*why?* Learning one rule for many words is much easier than learning each word individually. An index to these spelling rules is on page 239.

All examples and practice readings are included, which are *100% decodable*—comprised *only* of letters, sounds, and rules already learned. This reinforces and cements newly-learned skills, as well as developing accuracy and fluency. Using a piano analogy, just because a child knows the keyboard notes does not mean he is ready to play a lovely sonata! Similarly, just because a child knows letters and sounds does not mean he is ready to read good literature.

Large, 24 point letters are used for the text. Even with proper glasses students often struggle with smaller letters when learning. Once reading is established, it's easier to read finer print.

The diacritical markings used are consistent with those found in commonly used dictionaries. This knowledge is very handy for dictionary work later on. Using other notation systems will require relearning the dictionary's markings eventually. Why not learn them correctly first?

There is no guessing, and there is no choosing. Guessing is not the same as reading, and even considering a wrong answer takes unnecessary time and energy. What if a music teacher tried to teach you how to play the piano by having you choose the correct note from a list?

Younger children will enjoy Dewey the Bookworm as he guides them through these lessons. Older students and adults will find inspiration in the wise and humorous proverbs sprinkled throughout the book, encouraging virtues such as self-discipline, patience, perseverance, kindness, and personal integrity.

Phonics Pathways is approved for legal compliance with the California Department of Education, enabling school districts to purchase it with Instructional Materials Fund monies. It is an ideal complement to today's literature-based reading programs, providing the tools and teaching the skills needed to unlock and decode these wonderful, classic old stories.

William Blake once said:

*"There are things that are known
and things that are unknown…
and in between are only doors."*

Phonics Pathways is the key that will open the door to literacy for *everyone!*

TEACHING TIPS FOR REMEDIAL STUDENTS:

Use the review pages in the back of each lesson as a pre-test, in order to find out exactly where to begin these lessons. His starting point should be at the place he is able to work comfortably and accurately, from the very first day. Frequently students do not know the short-vowel sounds, or have difficulty blending sounds together. You will be able to determine this when pre-testing.

Tell him everyone needs help with something, and that many famous people had a lot of difficulty learning how to read and write. Explain that it *always* takes more time to unlearn something and re-learn it another way. Understanding these things will help him be a little more patient with himself.

Use imagery in creative ways. Many of the proverbs in *Phonics Pathways* were chosen especially to be encouraging and meaningful to remedial students—read them to him. Find out the things he enjoys doing, and talk about them. Remedial students need a lot of encouragement!

MORE BEGINNING STRATEGIES:

1. Using an overhead projector, have the whole class do the first two steps on page one together. Then call on individual students to say the name and beginning sound of the picture you point to—vary the picture, but always include the short sound of "A" as well.

2. Next, write a large "Aa" on the chalkboard. Trace each letter three times, naming its short sound out loud with the class each time. Repeat this exercise, this time having the students trace large letters on their desktop with their fingertips as you trace these letters on the board. Complete the remaining steps on page one, and repeat with the rest of the vowels.

3. Write all vowels in large letters in a horizontal line on the chalkboard and draw vertical lines between them. Dictate a vowel sound to your student and have him write it under the correct column, name it, and repeat the short sound of that vowel. (See also #2 on page 250.)

4. Make a master sheet with vowels in a horizontal line on top and vertical lines between them. Give a copy to each student. Dictate a sound, and ask students to write the letter in the correct column. Continue this exercise with blends and short-vowel words—it's great reinforcement!

5. Make a master sheet of the *Short-Vowel Stick* shown below. Run off enough copies for every student, laminate, and cut apart. Students should keep their *Short-Vowel Stick* on the desk at all times during reading lessons as a quick reference, It's an indispensable teaching tool!

6. Students enjoy using this *Short-Vowel Stick* as a bookmark as well, and also find it very handy to put underneath the word or sentence they are reading to help guide them across the page.

7. Be sure to check out all the tips, charts, activities, and games beginning on page 238! These reproducables are invaluable strategies that will greatly enhance your teaching in many different ways. The record-keeping sheets will prove very useful as well.

ant   exercise   itch   octopus   umbrella

SHORT-VOWEL SHUFFLE

The Short-Vowel Shuffle is played one-on-one with the teacher, in small groups, or with a whole class. This card game reviews and reinforces the short-vowel sounds, and is especially appropriate for younger students. Older students and adults will find these cards quite helpful used as flash cards to reinforce learning and speed up the recognition-response time. Either way, they are *very* helpful!

Copy this page, and run off four or more copies on colored cardstock. Laminate and cut apart. Begin with the **a** cards, and add more short-vowel cards as they are learned. Use all of the "eyes" cards. Shuffle the cards and place them face down on the middle of the table. Use several or many sets of cards, depending upon the number of vowels being played and how much time there is for playing.

1. Take turns drawing a card from the top of the stack. Students trace it with their fingertip (on the card or on their desktops), read the sound out loud, and lay it face up on the table.

2. Whenever an "eyes" card is turned over, one of the following things happens:
   (a) students "shuffle" once around their desk and sit down again (show them how to shuffle!),
   (b) teacher holds her nose and says "honk,"
   (c) students jump up and down like a jack-in-the-box,
   (d) whatever else was agreed upon beforehand—use your own imagination!

3. Continue playing the game until all of the cards have been drawn and read.

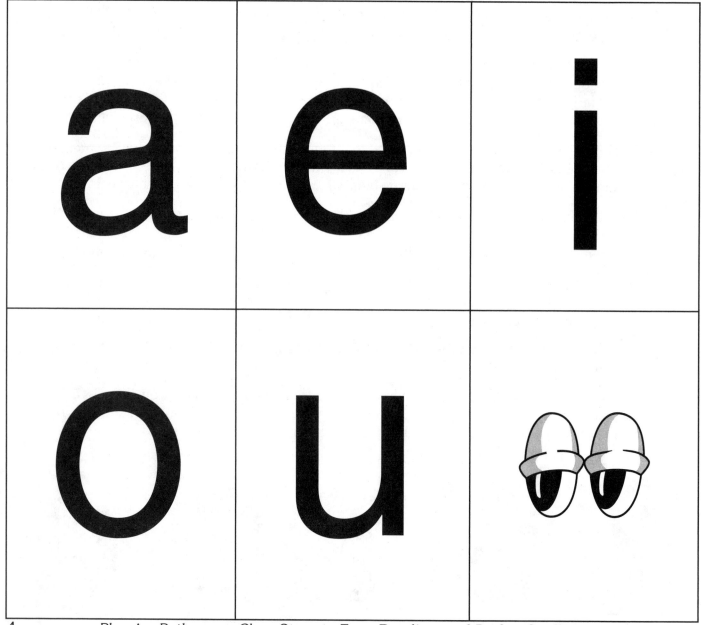

Phonics Pathways: Clear Steps to Easy Reading and Perfect Spelling

MISCELLANEOUS:

Exactly *how much* of this book must students learn in order to read, and *how long* will it take? Some students begin reading on their own very early in the book, while others need to learn many more rules and spelling patterns (*especially* students with learning disabilities) before being able to read with ease. It varies greatly.

This can be dramatically illustrated by looking at the results of a two-year pilot study using *Phonics Pathways* as an in-school tutoring program. Forty to sixty remedial students ranging from first to fourth grade participated. Parent volunteers tutored each student about three times a week, in twenty-minute sessions. These students required from 7 to 184 tutoring sessions in order to read at or near grade level. The following chart summarizes this activity:

Grade Level of Students	Skill Level Mastered Resulting in Reading at or Close to Grade Level	Page	Average No. of Tutoring Sessions
1st Grade	Two-Consonant Endings Review	67	50
2nd Grade	Long-Vowel Review	105	77
3rd & 4th Grade	Two-Consonant Beginnings Review	143	94

However, long after your student is reading, he should continue using this book for ongoing development and fluency in reading and spelling. Knowing these spelling rules, shortcuts, tips, and diacritical marks for dictionary work will give him a real "educational edge"!

While most students enjoy the humorous and encouraging proverbs, some of these sayings may be too sophisticated for the youngest ears to appreciate. You will be able to determine this as you work through the book.

Is your child clumsy, tired a lot, impulsive, and/or hyperactive? Does he have a short attention span and/or poor coordination? These children frequently have learning problems. Among the many causes for these symptoms *may* be allergies and sensitivities, which some specialists feel can take a systemic form instead of a more common, localized form such as hay fever. Experts disagree that this can be a factor. But you might consider asking your doctor for a safe elimination diet to try, and see if it makes a difference. At the very *least* you can try to avoid junk foods, or those with a lot of chemical additives. It makes a real difference with many children, and just might be worth trying!

Could he possibly have a vision problem, even though he may not need glasses? Some experts feel that if a child is clumsy and has poor coordination and/or reverses letters, he could also benefit from exercises designed to help eyes move together from left to right, and to improve motor coordination skills. The premise is that developing these skills is very helpful to the reading process. Experts disagree, but in my experience it has been beneficial to many students. Pages 246 and 247 contain some excellent and effective vision and motor coordination training exercises that are frequently prescribed by specialists when treating dyslexia. And, of course, left-to-right eye tracking is part of the teaching technique used throughout this book.

There will be many more teaching tips as you work through the book. Good luck, have fun, and remember—these times together should be an *enjoyable* learning experience for *both of you!*

Phonics Pathways: Clear Steps to Easy Reading and Perfect Spelling

ABOUT DEWEY

Dewey first made his appearance many years ago, in a secret note passed to my best friend Mary Lou in a third-grade classroom. At that time he was called "The Burp," and underwent many exciting adventures during the next few years before being retired for more worldly pursuits such as roller skating, fishing with Dad, reading fairy tales and Greek myths with Mom, and dressing up and parading around in my aunt's beautiful, sparkling, colorful old Ziegfeld Follies costumes found hidden in an old steamer trunk in a dusty corner of the attic.

The Burp was resurrected a few years ago when I was requested to design and create a large bookworm, to be submitted to the city wide Harvest Festival Doll competition representing the Livermore Public Library. He was carefully redesigned, receiving form and substance as a six-foot-tall pink and green fuzzy striped bookworm. Dewey D. System, Bookwormus Giganticus, was thrilled (and yes, a bit pompous!) when he won first prize.

Dewey and Kiwi

For a brief but glorious time Dewey reigned supreme high on a bookcase in the Friend's Corner of the Livermore Library, holding court with large throngs of admiring fans. He loved everyone, but *especially* the children. He tended to dissect and categorize when feeling playful, but pun terribly when feeling peevish. He fed late at night, long after the library had closed. He devoured books primarily, but was able to digest almost any variety of food for thought. Mostly he loved chewing on tasty, meaty things such as great big fat cookbooks, but confessed to nibbling spicy tidbits on the odd occasion. However, Dewey choked on political items of *any* flavor. For dessert he relished consuming dense, nutty but half-baked trifles, filled with dates.

Unfortunately, Dewey then began crunching Apples. He gobbled bits and bytes out of the mouse, ram, and any tasty cookie chips he found on the menu. Sad to say, he also sipped the port. He finally crashed with a system virus, and was politely requested to leave the library.

Dewey came back home to live, having earned a much-deserved and honorable retirement. He adores munching snacks and taking long naps with Kiwi, regaling her with tall tales about his glory days as a blue-ribbon prize winner. But sometimes—every once in a while—he gets a faraway look in his eyes, and seems a little sad and wistful. I wonder if, at those times, he might be dimly recalling those long-ago days when he was just a little Burp, sharing so many rousing adventures with two small, shy third-grade girls. I wonder…

What do *YOU* think?…*Dolores*

And now...

Whatever

you

CAN

do...

or DREAM

you

can...

BEGIN IT!

—Goethe

We shall begin by learning the *short sound* of the five vowels in the English language. We shall learn them one at a time, beginning with the letter "A." Try to spend just a few minutes, once or twice a day, learning these sounds.

1. *Listen carefully* while your teacher reads the name and beginning sound of each picture on the opposite page, including the letter "A." *Especially* notice the beginning sound. Try closing your eyes for better concentration:

> "Atom, ă; ant, ă; apple, ă; A, ă.
> Ă is the short sound of the letter A."

2. If you closed your eyes, now open them while she reads these pictures and sounds again. This time *you* say these pictures and sounds along with her:

> "Atom, ă; ant, ă; apple, ă; A, ă."

3. Read the name and short sound of "A," and *trace* each letter with your fingertip. Make sure you start at the correct place and move in the correct direction. Various writing pads or workbooks can show you how to do this.

4. Now *write* the letter and say this sound again. (If writing is too difficult: trace a big letter on the tabletop with your fingertip, trace an even bigger letter in the air with your fingertip, or just point to the sound being read. See page 247 for exercises that will help develop writing dexterity.)

5. Read the review in the window box at the bottom, then write it from dictation.

6. Play the *Short-Vowel Shuffle* on page 4. It helps you learn and is fun to play!

7. Repeat these instructions with each of the four remaining vowels.

And now—let us meet **DEWEY**,* a truly wise bookworm who will be your personal guide throughout this book. He adds his own inspiration and special thoughts to encourage you along the way.

> *Have you ever met a lot of people at the same time? It was very DIFFICULT to remember all of their names, wasn't it? Perhaps you couldn't. But when you meet people just ONE AT A TIME, it is so much easier.*
>
> *It is the same thing when learning how to read, or when learning how to do almost ANYTHING, for that matter. Just learn one small thing at a time, then another, and just keep on going. And before you know it, YOU will know it!*

*Dewey D. System, Bookwormus Giganticus ©1982 Dolores G. Hiskes

Phonics Pathways: Clear Steps to Easy Reading and Perfect Spelling

Aă Aă

There are TWO WAYS of writing "a."

Here is how we READ it: "a"

And here is how we WRITE it: "ɑ"

We need to know them BOTH.

"Atom, ă, apple, ă, ant, ă, A, ă"

The little mark you see above each of these letters is called a DIACRITICAL mark. This is the diacritical mark for a short-vowel sound. There are different marks for different sounds.

These marks tell you exactly how to pronounce letters and syllables. They are the *key* that shows you how to sound out a word when you look it up in the dictionary.

Knowing this code is *very handy!*

a   ɑ

Eĕ

...Hello!

...Hello!
If it's TOO HARD for you to hear these sounds clearly from dictation, try saying the sound out loud yourself, after hearing it. It may be helpful. Do this for as long as you need to.

Play the Short-Vowel Shuffle (page 4) with the "a" and "e" cards, and keep adding more letter cards as you learn them. It's a lot of FUN!

"Echo, ĕ, exercise, ĕ, evergreen, ĕ, edge, ĕ, E, ĕ."

Educators such as Maria Montessori have long known that when we use *all* of our senses to learn something, it easier to learn and remember. That is why we *see, hear, say, feel,* and *write* each letter that we are learning. This is called a MULTISENSORY method of learning, and it makes things so much easier. It's really amazing, when you stop to think about it!

a   e   a

Ĭĭ

It's REALLY DIFFICULT to tell these sounds apart at first.
Here's a NEAT TRICK that many people find very helpful (as well as fun!):

Let's suppose that you are having trouble being able to tell "i" from "e."
Try saying the "e" pictures using the "i" sound: "icho, ixercise, ivergreen, idge."
Now say the "i" pictures with the "e" sound: "etch, egloo." See what I mean?

This little ~~ixercise~~ exercise is helpful because when you listen to both the WRONG and RIGHT way of saying these sounds within a word, it is MUCH EASIER to hear the difference between them!

"Ĭtch, ĭ, igloo, ĭ, I, ĭ"

The *highest mountain*
    in the *whole world*
        is still climbed
            by taking only
one small step at a time, and keeping on going…

Just as *we* are learning how to *read* by taking only
one small step at a time, and keeping on going!

a e i a

Oŏ

It's MUCH easier to look at these short-vowel sounds JUST for a MINUTE, several times a day, than it is to have LONG study periods. After all, did YOU have to STUDY HARD to learn YOUR OWN NAME? Of course not! You learned it EASILY because you heard someone SAY it to you, off and on, each day since your birth.

Continue playing the Short-Vowel Shuffle. For added practice, put these letter-cards where you will see them a lot. Take a look at them every so often, and say them out loud. You will be SURPRISED at how QUICKLY you will learn them!

"Octopus, ŏ, ostrich, ŏ, O, ŏ."

The greatest book in the whole world
    begins with just *one word*…

And that word begins with only *one letter*.

So did *we* begin with only one letter!
Easy does it…slow but sure…we'll just take
    one small step at a time.

a e i o a

Uŭ

"Ugly, ŭ, up, ŭ, umbrella, ŭ, U, ŭ."

And that ends the vowels! On the next page is your first review. Remember one thing when reviewing: *Don't ever guess!* A wrong answer leaves an imprint on your brain, which then takes *more* time and energy to *unlearn*.

Always look back at the letter pictures until you know these sounds well enough not to. It makes things easier—and in the long run, you will learn *faster!*

a e i o u

BLENDIT! (Short-Vowel Review)

Review this page once a day, until this knowledge is second nature and automatic. When READING, name both the letter and its short sound. When WRITING, listen to the sound of the letter and then write down its name. Either read and write these letters directly from the page, or play one of the following vowel discrimination games for variety and fun: *Bingo*, numbers 3 and 4 on page 3, and numbers 1 and 2 on page 250.

Blendit! (similar to *Bingo*): Make three copies of this page. Use one copy for a board, and cut the other two copies into letter squares. Place the squares in a pile upside down in the middle of the table. Pick a card, read the sound out loud, and place it over the correct letter on the board. The first one to fill in all the letters in a row wins. Or, play until *both* players win—it's less pressure. (Also—*heh heh*—it's added practice. *Sneaky!*)

TEACHING TIPS: Pantomime a word for any sound your learner may have forgotten: bite an apple ("a"), lift an arm up and down ("e" exercise), scratch ("i" itch), wave arms around ("o" octopus), or point upwards ("u" up).

Look back at the letter pictures as often as necessary, but do not proceed until you know these sounds as well as you know your own name.

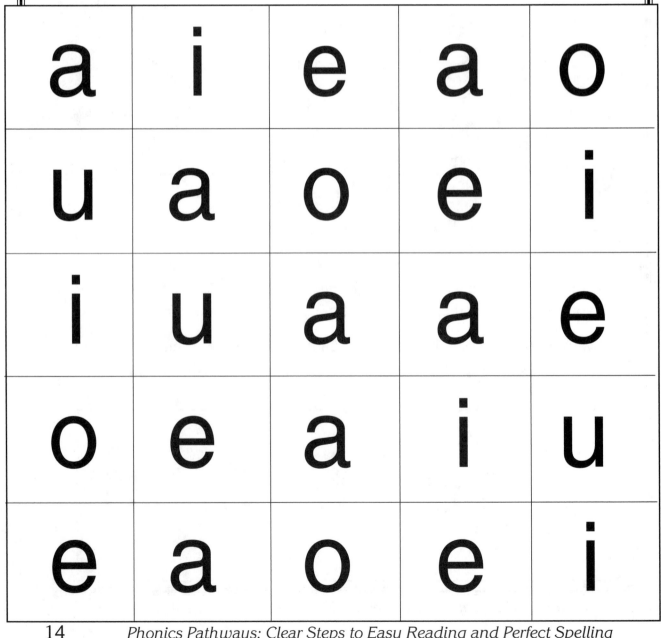

a	i	e	a	o
u	a	o	e	i
i	u	a	a	e
o	e	a	i	u
e	a	o	e	i

Now we shall learn some CONSONANTS and combine them with vowels to make two-letter blends. A consonant is any letter that is not a vowel.

Being able to blend letters together smoothly is a *very important skill!* It will train your eye muscles to track (move) together effortlessly from left to right across the page, so that you will be able to read words and books easily, without having to struggle. Blending practice is good exercise—it is aerobics for the eyes. In fact, let's call it *eye-robics* because that's what it is—aerobics for the eyes!

Eyerobics begins with seventeen pages of two-letter blends, gradually building up to long words made of many syllables. A syllable is the smallest part a word can be broken into which also contains a vowel—usually two or three-letter blends. We build bricks to make *houses*, and syllables to make *words*.

Blending exercises must be practiced in order to become automatic, just like any other skill such as riding a bicycle. For some students this will take longer than with others.

1—If blending is difficult:
Practice the blending game on page 18. This *Train Game* is extremely helpful to anyone needing help in learning this skill! There is also a master *Train Game* in the appendix on pages 253 and 254 that is blank, for those of you who wish to continue this exercise with other letters as well.

2—If blending is easy:
Skip *The Train Game* and continue the blending exercises until the end of this section of *Phonics Pathways*.

3—If blending is especially easy and effortless:
If blending is super-easy for you, *and* if you already know all the consonant sounds, you may skip the rest of the two-letter blend exercises and move on to the review on page 36. You can either read the blends as they are, or play *StarSearch* to review them for variety. It's good practice, and fun to play!

Did you know that sometimes very intelligent people can have real difficulty when learning how to blend letters together smoothly when reading?

Blending skills have nothing to do with intelligence any more than wearing glasses does!

DIRECTIONS:

1. Name each picture on the page, and listen for its beginning sound. Each picture begins with the sound of the consonant introduced on that page. (The names of these pictures also contain many sounds you have not had yet, but you *only* are to listen for the *beginning sound* of each one.)

2. Now *blend* the consonant sound with the vowel sound. Begin at the top of the ladder, and read the short "a." Then read the two sounds individually as you move across the page: "s—a." Now blend the two sounds together. Take a *DEEP BREATH* and *STRETCH* the sounds out as you read them, smoothly blending the sound of one vowel into the other:

$$\textit{"SSSSSaaaaaaaaaaa"}$$

3. Link this blend with a real word, such as "sa" as in "sat, Sam, sad," etc. Continue in this manner with the rest of the vowels, moving down the page.

4. Read the blends in the review window at the bottom. Keep your *Short-Vowel Stick* handy (page 3) as a quick reference to short-vowel sounds.

5. Write these sounds from dictation. (Remember, if you find it difficult to identify these sounds from dictation alone, say them to yourself first.)

6. Repeat these instructions with the rest of the consonants in this section,

7. If blending is too much of a challenge for you in the beginning, practice *The Train Game* on page 18. It's a hands-on activity that's *sure* to help!

Spend about ten minutes a day with this section. You might complete several pages in one day, or you might spend several days on one page. It is how much *time* you spend that counts, not how many *pages* that you do!

We review each step a LOT because we need to know this material at a deep level until it's automatic in recall, just as we know our own name. It's like learning how to ride a bicycle, or drive a car: At first, we need to go VERY SLOWLY and think about every step involved. We would NEVER think of going out on a busy freeway or down a steep hill our first time out. That comes later, when our skills are practiced enough to be automatic. THEN it's FUN!

Ss

a	s-a	sa
e	s-e	se
i	s-i	si
o	s-o	so
u	s-u	su

These exercises are excellent practice! But if this page is too DIFFICULT for you, play The Train Game on the next page first. Keep playing it until blending becomes easier for you. (On the other hand, if these pages seem too EASY for you, and if you already know the consonant sounds, you may proceed directly to the review on page 36.)

su	so	si	se	sa
se	su		so	si

Star, snowman, swan

The Train Game game provides intensive kinesthetic eye-tracking practice, helping to prevent or correct reversals. Copy and laminate this page, and cut the letters apart:

1– Place the "s" and "a" cars on the table, with the "s" car on your left and the "a" car on your right, about one or two feet apart.

2– "Chug" the "s" car slightly toward the center with your left hand. Look at it while you slide it, and say its sound at the same time.

3– Now focus your attention on the "a" car. Look at it and chug it slightly toward the center, saying its short sound while you are watching it.

4– Keep going in this fashion, until the cars meet. When the cars "hitch" together, the sounds should hitch together also, in one smooth blend. Be sure that you always *look* at each letter or blend while you *say* it.

(There is a master *Train Game* on pages 253-254 to use with other letters if desired.)

Mm

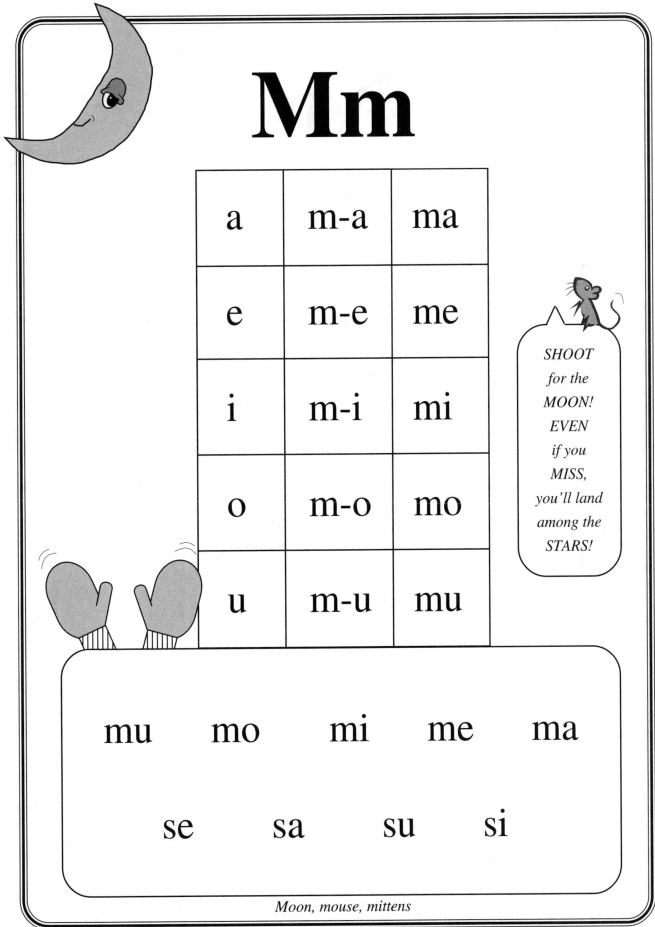

a	m-a	ma
e	m-e	me
i	m-i	mi
o	m-o	mo
u	m-u	mu

SHOOT for the MOON! EVEN if you MISS, you'll land among the STARS!

mu   mo   mi   me   ma

se   sa   su   si

Moon, mouse, mittens

Nn

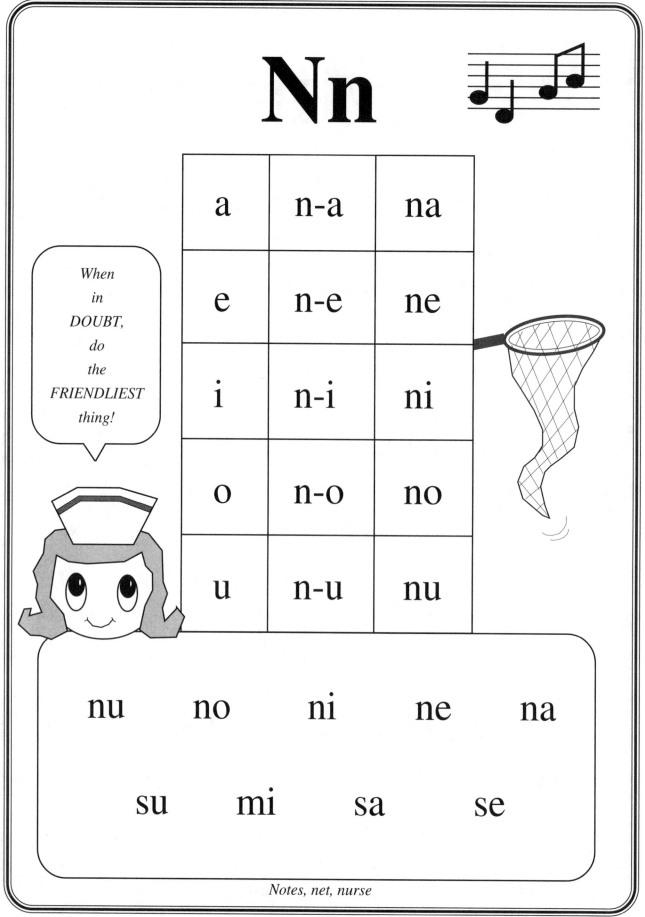

a	n-a	na
e	n-e	ne
i	n-i	ni
o	n-o	no
u	n-u	nu

When
in
DOUBT,
do
the
FRIENDLIEST
thing!

nu   no   ni   ne   na

su   mi   sa   se

Notes, net, nurse

Rr

a	r-a	ra
e	r-e	re
i	r-i	ri
o	r-o	ro
u	r-u	ru

EVERYONE has a RAINY CORNER in his life!

ru   ro   ri   re   ra

na   se   mu   ni

ra   ra-n   ran

Rain, ring, rabbit

Ll

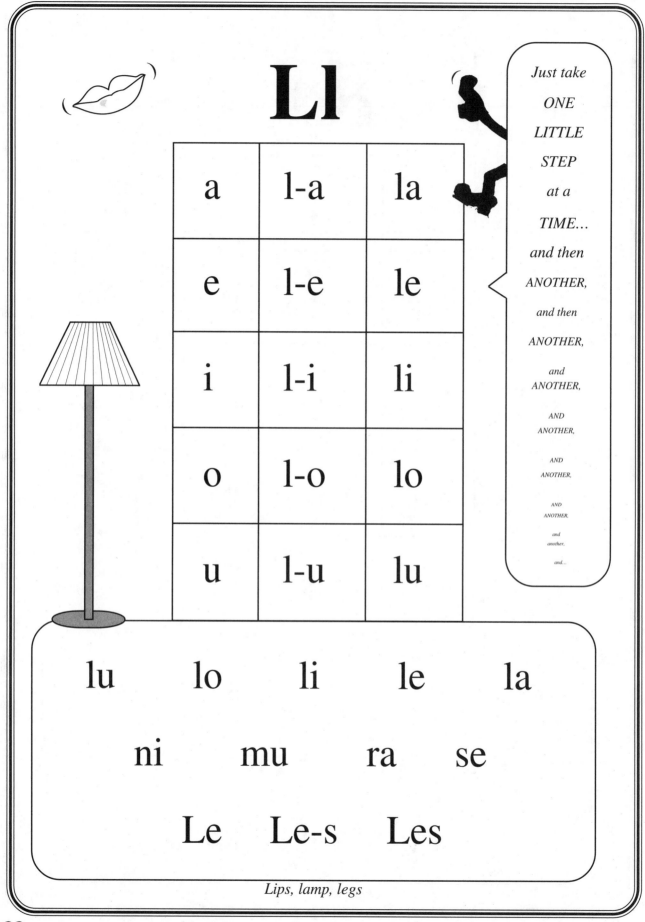

Just take
ONE
LITTLE
STEP
at a
TIME...
and then
ANOTHER,
and then
ANOTHER,
and
ANOTHER,
AND
ANOTHER,
AND
ANOTHER,
AND
ANOTHER,
and
another,
and...

a	l-a	la
e	l-e	le
i	l-i	li
o	l-o	lo
u	l-u	lu

lu   lo   li   le   la

ni   mu   ra   se

Le   Le-s   Les

Lips, lamp, legs

Ff

Remember—when reading these blends also think of some words that BEGIN with these sounds:

"fu" as in "fun," "fo" as in "fox," "fi" as in "fish," etc.

(How many different words can YOU think of?)

a	f-a	fa
e	f-e	fe
i	f-i	fi
o	f-o	fo
u	f-u	fu

fu	fo	fi	fe	fa
ru	se	lo	ni	
fu	fu-n	fun		

Flower, finger, fish

Phonics Pathways: Clear Steps to Easy Reading and Perfect Spelling   23

Hh

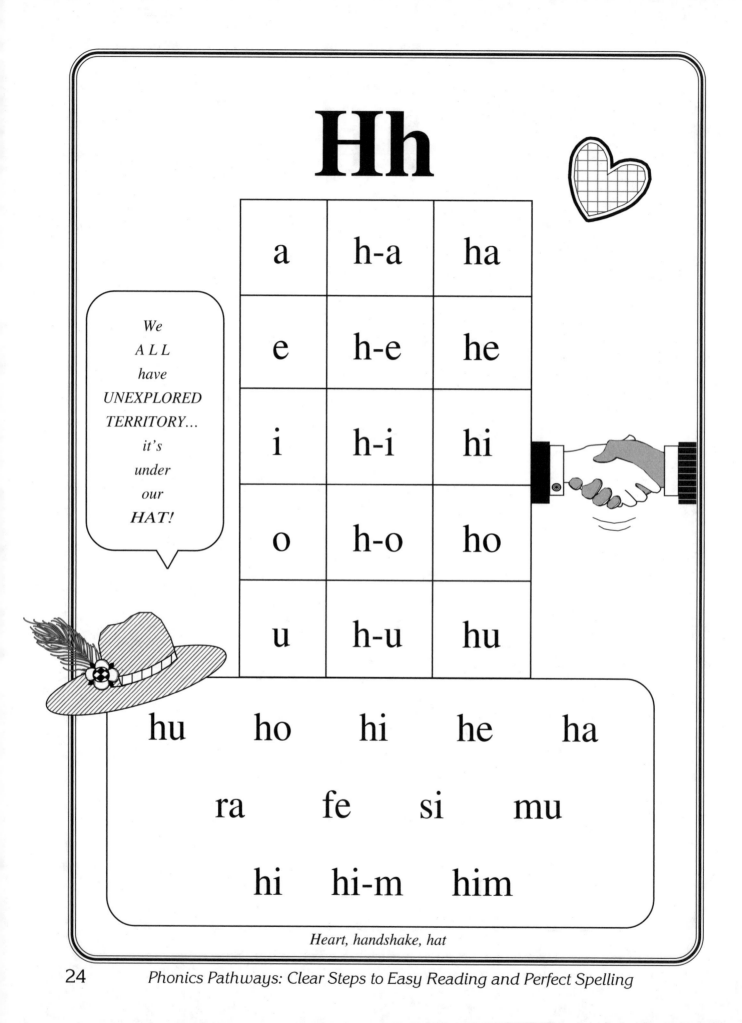

a	h-a	ha
e	h-e	he
i	h-i	hi
o	h-o	ho
u	h-u	hu

We
ALL
have
UNEXPLORED
TERRITORY...
it's
under
our
HAT!

hu   ho   hi   he   ha

ra   fe   si   mu

hi   hi-m   him

Heart, handshake, hat

Dd

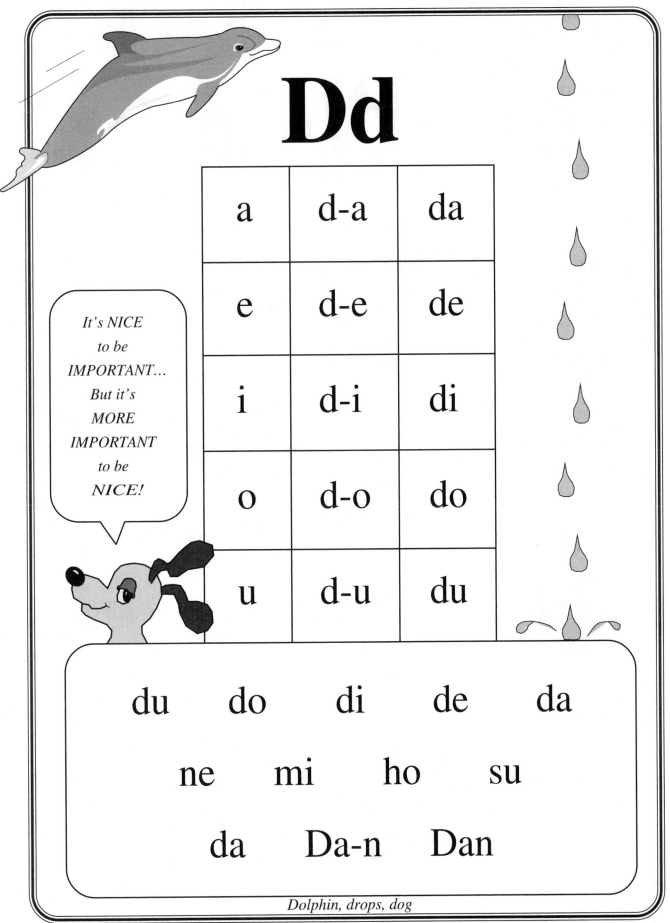

a	d-a	da
e	d-e	de
i	d-i	di
o	d-o	do
u	d-u	du

It's NICE to be IMPORTANT... But it's MORE IMPORTANT to be NICE!

du   do   di   de   da

ne   mi   ho   su

da   Da-n   Dan

Dolphin, drops, dog

Bb

It's MUCH BETTER to spend just a FEW MINUTES A DAY with this book, rather than studying LONGER, but only SEVERAL TIMES A WEEK. It's like brushing your teeth... They wouldn't look NEARLY as nice if you brushed them only TWICE A WEEK but for LONGER, would they?

a	b-a	ba
e	b-e	be
i	b-i	bi
o	b-o	bo
u	b-u	bu

bu   bo   bi   be   ba

du   ne   mi   fa

bu   bu-n   bun

Bees, bear, butterfly

Pp

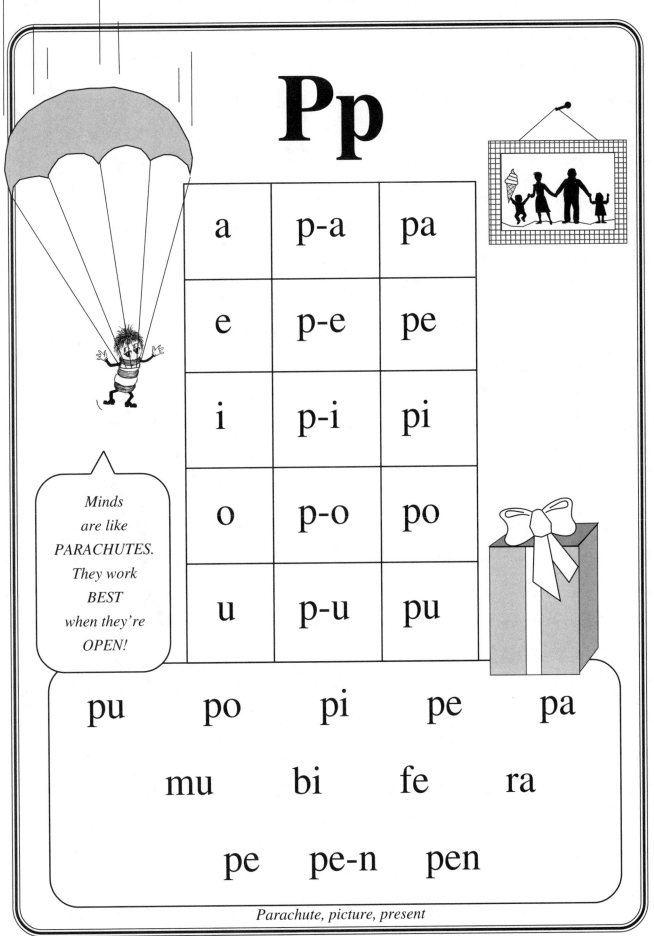

a	p-a	pa
e	p-e	pe
i	p-i	pi
o	p-o	po
u	p-u	pu

Minds are like PARACHUTES. They work BEST when they're OPEN!

pu	po	pi	pe	pa
mu	bi	fe		ra
pe	pe-n	pen		

Parachute, picture, present

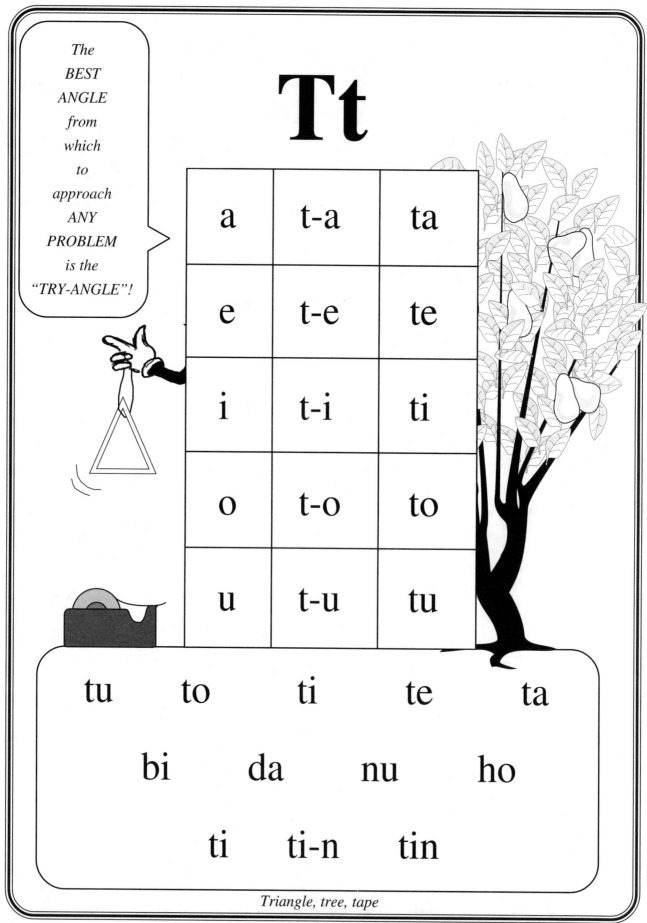

Tt

a	t-a	ta
e	t-e	te
i	t-i	ti
o	t-o	to
u	t-u	tu

tu	to	ti	te	ta
bi	da	nu	ho
ti	ti-n	tin

Triangle, tree, tape

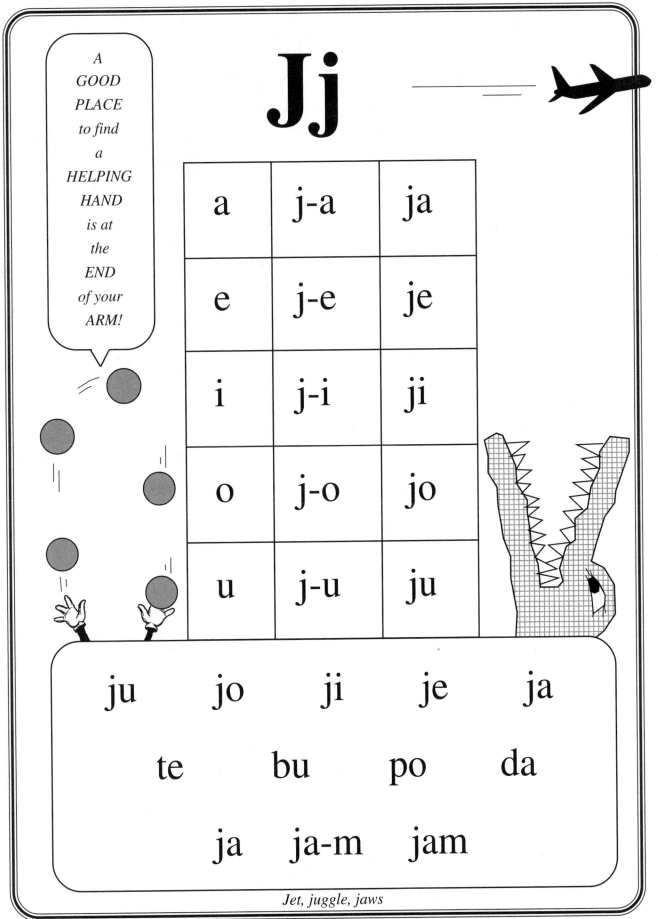

Jj

A GOOD PLACE to find a HELPING HAND is at the END of your ARM!

a	j-a	ja
e	j-e	je
i	j-i	ji
o	j-o	jo
u	j-u	ju

ju	jo	ji	je	ja
te	bu	po	da
ja	ja-m	jam

Jet, juggle, jaws

Gg Gg

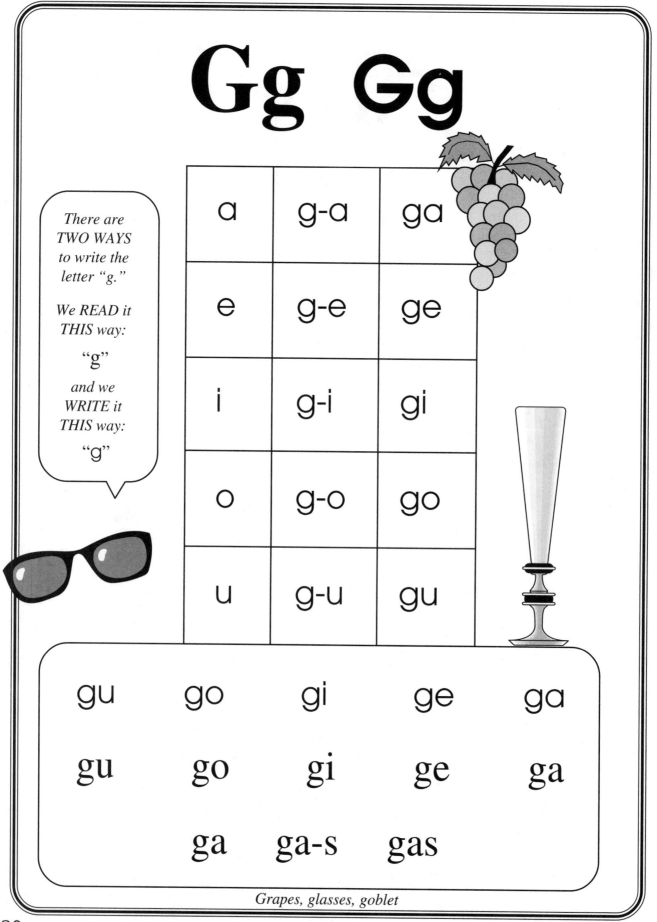

There are *TWO WAYS to write the letter "g."*

We READ it THIS way:

"g"

and we WRITE it THIS way:

"g"

a	g-a	ga
e	g-e	ge
i	g-i	gi
o	g-o	go
u	g-u	gu

gu	go	gi	ge	ga
gu	go	gi	ge	ga

ga	ga-s	gas

Grapes, glasses, goblet

Phonics Pathways: Clear Steps to Easy Reading and Perfect Spelling

Vv

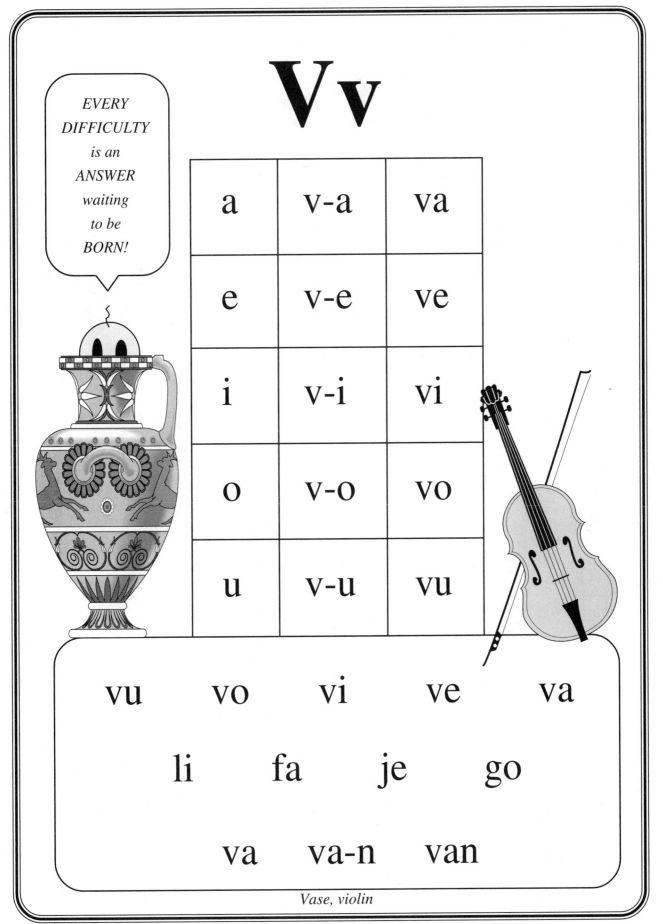

a	v-a	va
e	v-e	ve
i	v-i	vi
o	v-o	vo
u	v-u	vu

vu   vo   vi   ve   va

li   fa   je   go

va   va-n   van

Vase, violin

Ww

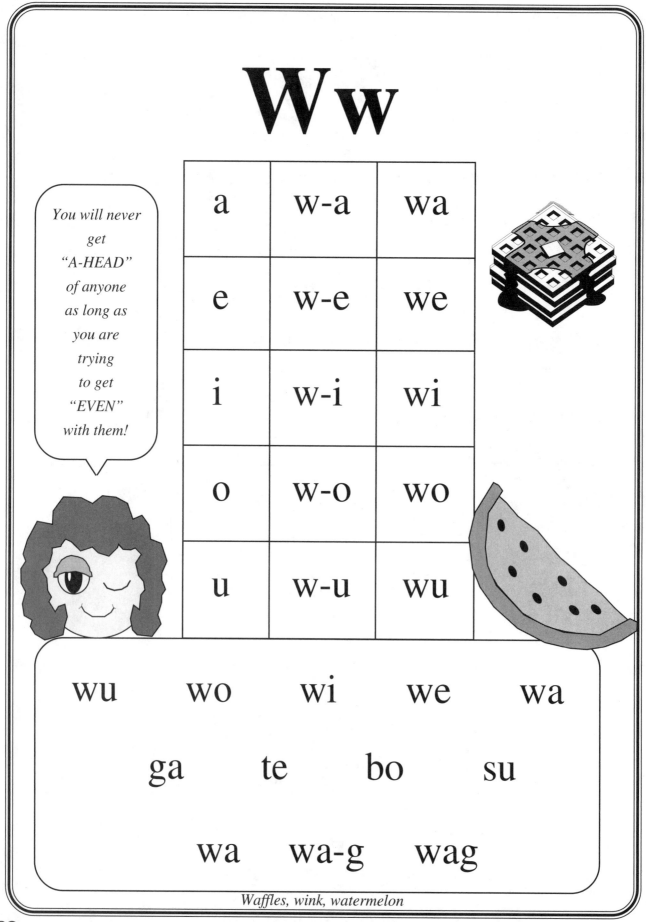

You will never get "A-HEAD" of anyone as long as you are trying to get "EVEN" with them!

a	w-a	wa
e	w-e	we
i	w-i	wi
o	w-o	wo
u	w-u	wu

wu   wo   wi   we   wa

ga   te   bo   su

wa   wa-g   wag

Waffles, wink, watermelon

Yy

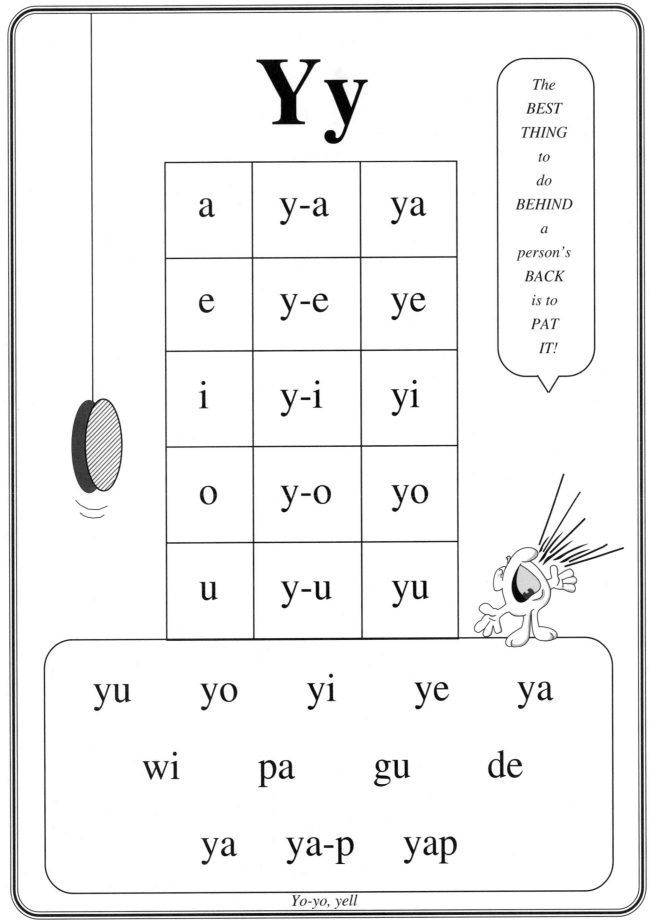

a	y-a	ya
e	y-e	ye
i	y-i	yi
o	y-o	yo
u	y-u	yu

The BEST THING to do BEHIND a person's BACK is to PAT IT!

yu   yo   yi   ye   ya

wi   pa   gu   de

ya   ya-p   yap

Yo-yo, yell

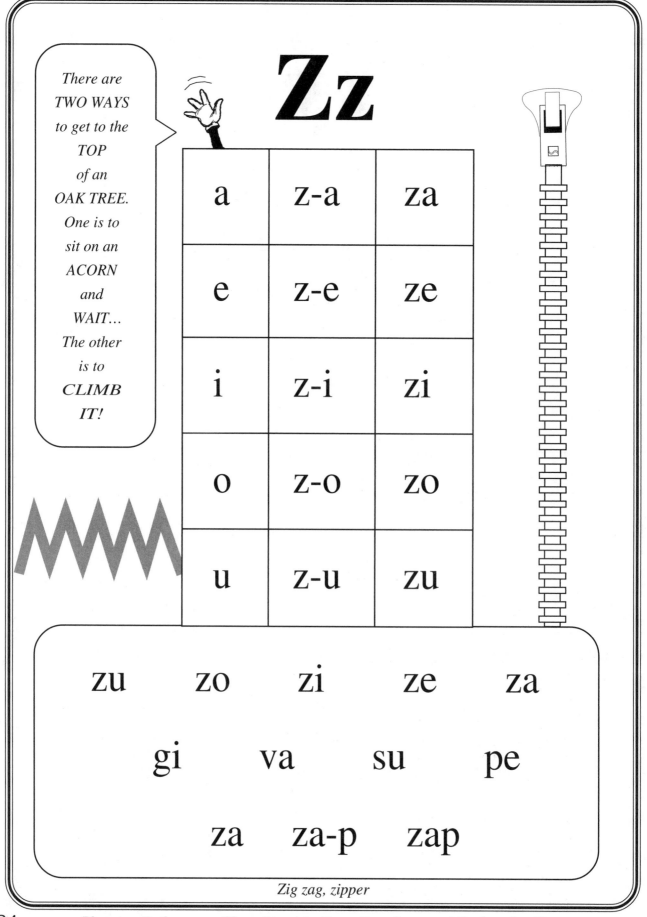

Zz

There are **TWO WAYS** to get to the **TOP** of an **OAK TREE.** One is to sit on an **ACORN** and **WAIT...** The other is to **CLIMB IT!**

a	z-a	za
e	z-e	ze
i	z-i	zi
o	z-o	zo
u	z-u	zu

zu   zo   zi   ze   za

gi   va   su   pe

za   za-p   zap

Zig zag, zipper

TWO-LETTER BLEND REVIEW

You may review these blends either by reading them directly or by playing *StarSearch* on the following page. (There is a master *StarSearch* in the index if you would like to continue playing this game with future lessons.)

Read and write these blends once a day until you can do so easily. (Either write them from dictation, or copy them after reading them if writing is too much of a challenge just yet.)

And remember: It isn't enough just to sound out each letter individually, as in "s—a", you must blend them both together into one smooth sound:

"*sssssaaaaaaaaaaa*"

Look back at the letter pictures as often as you need to, so that you are *thinking it through*, and *not guessing!*

STARSEARCH (Master copy on page 256)

1—Make several copies of the *StarSearch* game on the next page, on cardstock. Copy, laminate and cut apart all of the cards.

2—Place as many letters and stars cards as you wish to play with on the middle of the table in a pile, upside down. Shuffle to mix them up.

3—Take turns drawing a card and reading it out loud, blending the letters together in one smooth blend.

4—Return all letter cards to the table, but keep the stars cards you pick up. The player with the most stars cards wins!

TEACHING TIPS:

(1) When writing these lessons, try using a whiteboard with a dry-erase marking pen. It's easy to wipe clean and try again when first learning!

(2) Having trouble tell ing "b" from "d"? Make a copy of this "bed" card, and keep it handy as a quick reference. The "b" MUST go to the RIGHT and the "d" MUST go to the LEFT in order to hold the mattress up!

bed

se	fa	ro	hu
mi	ta	di	bo
na	pe	gi	ju
yu	ba	de	zi
le	vo	wu	po

Phonics Pathways: Clear Steps to Easy Reading and Perfect Spelling

Eyerobics continues by adding consonants to the end of two-letter blends to build three-letter words, and then combining two words to make a phrase.

Read each sound and blend, working across the page. When these blends are written with a line between them like this, "s-a," read each sound separately. When they are written without a line between them, as in "sa," you must *blend* the sounds together *smoothly.* It can help to take a deep breath first.

Take all the time you need in order to read each three-letter word *without* having to sound out individual letters first. The time this takes will vary; it depends upon how soon your eye muscles are strong enough to "track" across a word. It does *not* depend upon how *smart* you are!

Now listen to these words and write them from dictation. Try writing the two-word phrases from dictation also; but if that is too difficult just yet, your teacher can dictate these words one at a time. And if dictation is still difficult, then copy them from the page—just the actual word will do, not the two-letter blend.

Work about ten minutes a day with these lessons. Take all the time you need in order to read these words *without* having to sound out each letter first.

T E A C H I N G   T I P S : Do your eyes sometimes "skip" and "jump around" when reading? Put the *Short-Vowel Stick* or a sheet of paper underneath the *line* you are reading and move your finger underneath each *word* as you read it.

Still having trouble? Try this: Cut out a rectangle in a plain sheet of paper, about 3/8 inches high by 6 inches wide. Lay it over the page, so that only the line you are trying to read is showing through the little "window." These little tricks can make reading a *lot* easier! Use them as long as you find it helpful.

Can't wait to read "real books?" Please finish these lessons at least through page 49 *before* trying to read books! Even the best of phonics readers have some sight words in them, and while some students have no trouble with this many others do. Remedial readers especially need to have phonics skills firmly established prior to combining phonetically decodable words with sight words. It's safe to say that most students should be able to read the pyramid on page 50 before moving on to real readers. After that, students may begin with simple highly-decodable readers, as desired and if it is not a struggle.

*Do you know
the definition of PATIENCE?
PATIENCE is being able to
IDLE YOUR MOTOR
when you REALLY feel like
STRIPPING YOUR GEARS!*

Reading across the page, slowly blend these letters into three-letter words. Then read the two-word phrases. (A phrase is just a part of a sentence.)

Now copy or write a few words from dictation, if you can—or you might even try writing a phrase! (If you find this page helpful, there are more exercises like this on page 248.)

If you still find blending a challenge, continue playing The Train Game on pages 253-254. It will help a lot, and make it much easier to acquire this skill!

a	s-a	sa	sa-t	sat
e	s-e	se	se-t	set
i	s-i	si	si-p	sip
o	s-o	so	so-b	sob
u	s-u	su	su-n	sun

sis sat   sun set

a e i o u

a	j-a	ja	ja-m	jam
e	j-e	je	je-t	jet
i	J-i	Ji	Ji-m	Jim
o	j-o	jo	jo-g	jog
u	j-u	ju	ju-g	jug

Jim jog   jam jug

Ss

sa	sa-d	sad
se	se-t	set
si	si-t	sit
so	so-b	sob
su	su-n	sun

Ff

fa	fa-d	fad
fe	fe-d	fed
fi	fi-n	fin
fo	fo-p	fop
fu	fu-n	fun

Rr

ra	ra-p	rap
re	re-d	red
ri	ri-b	rib
ro	ro-t	rot
ru	ru-g	rug

Hh

ha	ha-t	hat
he	he-n	hen
hi	hi-d	hid
ho	ho-t	hot
hu	hu-g	hug

sun fun   red hat

Mm

ma	ma-n	man
me	me-t	met
mi	mi-d	mid
mo	mo-p	mop
mu	mu-g	mug

Nn

na	na-g	nag
ne	ne-t	net
ni	ni-p	nip
no	no-d	nod
nu	nu-t	nut

Dd

da	da-d	dad
de	de-n	den
di	di-g	dig
do	do-t	dot
du	du-d	dud

Bb

ba	ba-d	bad
be	be-t	bet
bi	bi-g	big
bo	bo-p	bop
bu	bu-n	bun

*You can't be a SMART COOKIE
With a CRUMMY ATTITUDE!*

big mug   dig nut

Tt

ta	ta-p	tap
te	te-n	ten
ti	ti-n	tin
to	to-p	top
tu	tu-g	tug

Pp

pa	pa-n	pan
pe	pe-n	pen
pi	pi-n	pin
po	po-t	pot
pu	pu-n	pun

Gg

ga	ga-p	gap
ge	ge-t	get
gi	gi-g	gig
go	go-t	got
gu	gu-m	gum

Jj

ja	ja-m	jam
je	je-t	jet
Ji	Ji-m	Jim
jo	jo-g	jog
ju	ju-g	jug

jam pot   top jet

Ll

la	la-p	lap
le	le-g	leg
li	li-p	lip
lo	lo-t	lot
lu	lu-g	lug

Vv

va	va-n	van
va	va-t	vat
ve	ve-t	vet
vi	vi-m	vim

Our lives would run a lot more smoothly if SECOND THOUGHTS came FIRST!

Ww

wa	wa-g	wag
we	we-t	wet
we	we-b	web
wi	wi-n	win
wi	wi-g	wig

Yy

ya	ya-m	yam
ya	ya-p	yap
ye	ye-t	yet
yi	yi-p	yip
yu	yu-m	yum

win van   lug yam

Aa

da	da-d	dad
na	na-g	nag
sa	sa-p	sap
ra	ra-n	ran
ma	ma-d	mad

Ee

pe	pe-p	pep
be	be-g	beg
te	te-n	ten
ge	ge-t	get
ne	ne-t	net

Ii

si	si-s	sis
di	di-p	dip
bi	bi-t	bit
wi	wi-n	win
fi	fi-g	fig

*JUMPING TO CONCLUSIONS
is not HALF as good exercise
as DIGGING FOR FACTS!*

Oo

to	to-t	tot
mo	mo-p	mop
ro	ro-t	rot
ho	ho-t	hot
do	do-t	dot

Uu

pu	pu-p	pup
fu	fu-n	fun
su	su-b	sub
ru	ru-n	run
du	du-g	dug

Once a day, read and write as many groups of words as you are able to do comfortably. First read *down* each group. Then read these words again, this time reading *across* the page. This is a little bit more difficult, and you might find yourself reading more slowly. (Also: be *sure* to check out the activities and games beginning on page 250 for review!)

dad	bet	bin	hop	bug
had	get	din	mop	hug
mad	met	fin	top	dug
sad	pet	win	lop	mug

bag	bed	did	nod	fun
nag	fed	hid	rod	bun
tag	red	rid	sod	run
sag	led	lid	pod	sun

lap	beg	nip	dot	but
nap	leg	rip	hot	hut
map	peg	tip	not	gut
gap	Meg	sip	lot	nut

The person who FOLLOWS THE CROWD usually will get NO FURTHER!

Read across the page:

tag nag	get pet	hug bug
hid lid	red bed	hop top
rip tip	hot lot	nap lap
nut hut	sad dad	fun run
beg Meg	win fin	nod rod

Read down each group of words first, and then read them across the page. Try copying or writing some of these words from dictation also—perhaps about five to ten words. Writing words helps you remember them better!

bat	den	big	rum	ham
fat	hen	dig	gum	jam
hat	men	pig	hum	Pam
rat	pen	wig	sum	Sam
Pat	ten	rig	mum	yam

dip	jug	him	ban	bit
hip	lug	Jim	fan	fit
lip	pug	dim	man	hit
zip	rug	rim	pan	sit
tip	tug	Tim	ran	pit

Becoming educated is getting to know all of the things you DIDN'T KNOW that you DIDN'T KNOW!

FAMOUS BOOKWORMS I HAVE KNOWN

The vowels in each phrase are the same. Read across:

fat bat	ten men	big rig
hum sum	yam jam	lug jug
tan van	den pen	pig dig
tug rug	Pat hat	dim rim
rum gum	Sam ham	man ran

You may review these words either by reading them directly from the opposite page, or by playing *Bag The Bugs* with the cards, as directed below. (There is a master *Bag The Bugs* in the appendix if you would like to continue playing this game with other lessons.)

First read them, then write them from dictation. Copy them if dictation is too difficult at this time. If you still have trouble writing, just trace a few of these words on the desktop with your fingertip. Reading skills frequently develop faster than writing skills, and we don't want to hold you back.

If you still need to sound out each letter individually, please read that word again. This time blend all letters together into *one smooth sound.* Blending skills are so important!

BAG THE BUGS
(Needs a box with lid.)

1—Make several copies of the *Bag The Bugs* game on the opposite page on cardstock. Laminate and cut apart all of the cards.

2—Place cards face down on the table. Students take turns drawing a card and reading the words. When a bug card turns up, student quickly puts the card in the box and slams the top down so the bug won't sting him! Play until cards are gone, and all players are "safe!"

3—Alternatively, keep any bug card that is drawn, and the player with the most bug cards after all the cards have been played is the winner.

(A master copy of *Bag The Bugs* is on page 257 if you wish to continue playing this game with other lessons.)

Take your time, and don't worry about making a mistake.
It's not whether you stumble or fall that matters…
What matters is that you just get up and keep on going.
Sometimes it's the last key in the bunch that opens the lock!

bug hop	Jim hum	mad Meg	wet gum
sun hat	big man	mop van	nip Dan
fig jam	Pat run	zip bag	hot mug
beg Nan	fat pig	get cat	fed Gus
Ned jog	red jug	tip top	pup hid

I get.
I get wet.

I had.
I had fun.

I bet.
I bet Dad.

I got.
I got jam.

I sip.
I sip pop.

I hug.
I hug Mom.

I win.
I win a van.

I pet.
I pet a pig.

I pop.
I pop a bag.

I ran.
I ran a bit.

I dug.
I dug an ant.

I sit.
I sit a lot.

hug pup	I hug a pup.
wet pup	I hug a wet pup.
big pup	I hug a big, wet pup!
fed pig	I fed a pig.
fat pig	I fed a fat pig.
big pig	I fed a big, fat pig!
met elf	I met an elf.
sad elf	I met a sad elf.
big elf	I met a big, sad elf!

jog bit	I jog a bit.
hop lot	I hop a lot.
	I jog a bit and hop a lot!
mop bit	I mop a bit.
run lot	I run a lot.
	I mop a bit and run a lot!
sip bit	I sip a bit.
sup lot	I sup a lot.
	I sip a bit and sup a lot!

To AVOID that RUN DOWN feeling... CROSS STREETS CAREFULLY! (Read across the page.)

PYRAMID (See also pages 248-249)

Pyramid is an enjoyable game that will help you read sentences a little easier. It bridges the gap between reading *whole words* and reading *longer sentences*. This is an excellent way to strengthen your eye tracking and increase your eye span—and besides, it is a lot of fun!

Read each line across the page, beginning with the very top word. At first, you are *not expected* to be able to read the longer sentences at the bottom of the page. In time, and with practice, you will be able to read these long sentences. (Remember to put a sheet of paper under the line you are reading, if this has been helpful.)

Now try *writing* these phrases from dictation, beginning at the top, to see how many words you are able to remember at one time. Practicing this will develop your *auditory* ability to recall images sequentially, just as playing *Memory* will help develop your *visual* memory skills (see "Getting Started," page 2).

Keep practicing with *Pyramid* to develop your eye-tracking skills. It will help you be able to read the sentences in these lessons much more easily. Sooner or later you will be able to read *anything!* It just takes time and practice. There is an additional *Pyramid* in the back of the book, on pages 248 and 249. Read it, as well. *Pyramids* are excellent "warm-ups" for all of the lessons to come!

And now—here is a secret of how to have a *really good* lesson: You must proceed *fast* enough to hold your interest, otherwise you may become *bored,* but *slowly* enough to experience success, otherwise you may become *frus-trated*. Everyone must find his or her very own pace… *you find yours!*

sip

Sip pop.

Jan sips pop.

Jan sits and sips pop.

Jan sits in sun and sips pop.

Jan sits in sun and sips pop in a mug.

Jan sits in hot sun and sips pop in a big mug.

Jan sits in hot sun and sips hot pop in a big mug!

The "k" sound can be spelled in different ways! Here are two spellings:

1–At the beginning of a word it is usually spelled "k" if the following letter is "e" or "i," as in "keg" or "kid."

2–If the following letter is any other vowel, it is usually spelled "c" as in "cat," "cot," or "cup."

The diacritical mark for this sound is simply "k."

Cc, Kk

a	c-a	ca
e	k-e	ke
i	k-i	ki
o	c-o	co
u	c-u	cu

It's "k" and not "c" with an "i" or an "e"!

cu   co   ki   ke   ca

ki   ca   cu   co

Cat, kite, cake, cup

Read down each set of words:

ca-t cat   ke-g keg
ca-n can   Ke-n Ken
ca-p cap
ca-d cad   ki-d kid
ca-b cab   ki-ss kiss
ca-m cam   ki-t kit

co-p cop   cu-p cup
co-t cot   cu-t cut
co-d cod   cu-b cub

*Each day is
MADE
SPECIAL
by what we can
GIVE
it…
by how we
ACCEPT
it
and how we
LIVE IN
it!*

Read across the page:

can	cat	cap	cab	Cass
keg	Ken	cad	cup	cop
kit	kiss	Kim	kid	kill
cod	cot	con	cob	cog
cub	cud	cup	cuff	cut

Ken cup   kid Cass   cab cut

Kit can   kiss cat   cop cap

The "k" sound at the *end* of a short-vowel single-syllable word is usually spelled "ck." (See page 113 for definition of syllables.) Read across the page:

k=-ck

so-ck	sock	sa-ck	sack
ti-ck	tick	to-ck	tock
du-ck	duck	su-ck	suck
bu-ck	buck	lu-ck	luck
Ri-ck	Rick	si-ck	sick
pi-ck	pick	Ni-ck	Nick
Ja-ck	Jack	pa-ck	pack
ra-ck	rack	ro-ck	rock

Reading across the page, only the *beginning letters* of the words are different:

a	rack	Jack	back	sack	hack	lack
e	deck	beck	peck	neck	peck	deck
i	pick	sick	tick	Nick	kick	lick
o	rock	sock	dock	hock	lock	jock
u	suck	tuck	luck	muck	duck	buck

pick Rick	back pack	luck suck
tuck buck	kick Nick	lack sack
mock jock	Jack back	Rick sick
lock dock	peck neck	duck muck

These "k" words are all *different*. Read across the page: (Also, remember to check out some of the great tips and games found from page 250 on!)

kiss cat	mock Rick	lick keg
pick lock	Jack can	Kip hock
duck peck	lack buck	cut sock
kick cot	pick sack	cap rack
back pack	lick cup	tick tock
lock deck	tuck neck	Kim luck
nick jock	Ken sick	suck rock

The only thing wrong with doing NOTHING is that you NEVER KNOW when you are FINISHED!

These words combine the "c-k-ck" sound with lessons previously learned:

miss Jack	get rock	kid Nan
pick fig	duck bit	fat sock
pack rug	cut sack	pig lick
tuck Don	Jack sat	lug rock
mop back	lack wig	bad luck
Kim ran	Rick hop	hug cat
kick bug	jog back	tug pack
pug wag	lack nut	cup rack

nick cup	I nick a hot cup.
lack sock	I lack a red sock.
duck peck	A duck can peck!
Ken back	Ken is back in bed.
pack sack	I can pack a big sack.
kiss sick	I kiss a sad, sick cat.
Jack back	Jack had a back deck.
kick rock	I can kick a big rock.

Review these words once a day. Read as many as you can. Now write some of them from dictation as well.

From now on copy or write about five or ten words, or three to six phrases and sentences, as an ongoing part of every lesson for the rest of this book. (At least try writing them—but if it slows you down too much, then just trace them with your fingertip for awhile.)

Practice until you are able to read these words effortlessly and smoothly, and spell them correctly.

Try to do something every day, even though you may not always feel like it. Think of it this way:

A DIAMOND is nothing but a piece of COAL
that MADE GOOD under PRESSURE!

Now you are ready for *four-letter* words! Working from left to right, read the two-letter blend, then the three-letter blend, and finally the four-letter word. To begin with, these words will be broken down as follows. Read across the page:

sa	san	san-d	sand
fe	fel	fel-t	felt

You should be able to read the three-letter blend *smoothly*, add the last letter, and then read the *whole word* in *one smooth blend.* Read (and then write if you can) as many words as you are able to each day.

T E A C H I N G T I P S: After the next two pages, these words will not be broken down as above. If some of them should be difficult to read, it can be *very* helpful to cover up the last letter with a piece of paper, read the three-letter blend, uncover the letter, and then read the whole word:

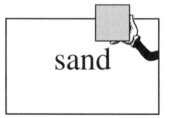

Do this as often as you need to in order to read these words smoothly. If these words continue to be difficult for you, just stay with the three-letter-word section of the book for a while to build up your reading skills until you are able to read these four-letter words a little bit more easily. Remember—there is *no hurry!*

Try reading the little "stories" in the window boxes. They contain only words made of letters that you have already learned, and are a good introduction to "real reading." If this is easy for you, it might be a good time to try some beginning phonics readers.

However, if these stories are too difficult to read just yet, then read only the words to the left of each sentence, and try to follow along with your eyes as your teacher *slowly* reads these sentences and underlines each word with her finger.

R E M E M B E R: If your eyes "skip around" while reading, hold the *Short-Vowel Stick* or a piece of paper underneath the line you are reading, or cut out a rectangle from a plain piece of paper as described on page 37. Do this for as long as you find it helpful.

T H I N K A B O U T I T: After you read each little story, discuss it with your teacher. Who were the characters? What happened in the story? It's important not only *to be able* to read, but *to understand* what you are reading!

is	his	is
is mad	his bed	jet is
is mad as	his bed has	his jet is
as	has	as
as hot	pup has	bad as
as hot as	his pup has	as bad as

Now let's give some four-letter words a try! Read across the page:

| fe | fel | fel-t | felt |
| sa | san | san-d | sand |

| fel-t | Ben felt. |
| san-d | Ben felt sand. |

| ru | run | run-s | runs |
| fa | fas | fas-t | fast |

| run-s | Ben runs. |
| fas-t | Ben runs fast on sand. |

ru	run	run-t	runt
he	hel	hel-d	held
te	ten	ten-t	tent

run-t	Ben has a runt pet pig.
hel-d	Ben held his pet pig, Gus.
ten-t	Gus is as fat as a big tent!

ro	rom	rom-p	romp
ju	jum	jum-p	jump
re	res	res-t	rest

There's only ONE THING that S I T S its way to success... a CHICKEN!

rom-p	Ben and Gus romp.
jum-p	Ben and Gus run and jump.
fas-t	Ben runs fast but Gus puffs a lot!

mi	mil	mil-k	milk
lu	lum	lum-p	lump
fe	fel	fel-t	felt

mil-k	Ben and Gus sip hot milk.
lum-p	Gus has a lump in his milk.
min-t	His lump is a big, fat mint.
bes-t	Gus yells, "Mint milk is best!"

Ss

sa	sap	
se	set	
si	sip	
so	sob	
su	sum	
sa	san	sand
se	sen	send

Mm

ma	man	
me	met	
mi	mid	
mo	mop	
mu	mud	
mi	mis	mist
mi	mil	milk

Ll

la	lan	land
le	len	lend
li	lis	list
lo	lof	loft
lu	lum	lump
li	lim	limp

Ff

fa	fas	fast
fe	fen	fend
fi	fis	fist
fo	fon	fond
fu	fun	fund
fe	fel	felt

Ben felt	Ben felt sand.
his sand	His sand is hot.
runs fast	Ben runs fast on hot sand.

Bb

ba	ban	band
be	ben	bend
bi	bil	bilk
bo	bon	bond
bu	bus	bust
be	bes	best

Rr

ra	ram	ramp
re	res	rest
ri	rif	rift
ro	rom	romp
ru	rus	rust
ra	raf	raft

Dd

da	dam	damp
de	des	desk
di	dis	disk
du	dum	dump
de	den	dent
du	dus	dust

Hh

ha	han	hand
he	hel	held
hi	hin	hint
hu	hus	husk
hu	hun	hunt
hu	hul	hulk

KEEP your TEMPER... nobody ELSE wants it!

Ben kept	Ben kept a pet pig.
held Gus	Ben held Gus, his pet pig.
romp hunt	Gus and Ben romp and hunt.

Phonics Pathways: Clear Steps to Easy Reading and Perfect Spelling

Gg

ga   gas   gasp
gu   gul   gulp
gu   gus   gust

Tt

ta   tas   task
te   ten   tent
tu   tus   tusk

Pp

pe   pes   pest
pu   pum   pump
pe   pen   pent

Kk

ki   kil   kilt
ke   kep   kept
ke   kel   kelp

Jj

ju   jus   just
ju   jum   jump
je   jes   jest

Ww

we   wep   wept
wi   wim   wimp
wi   win   wind

Not everyone at this point will need to read the two-letter blends first. If you still tend to reverse letters or words, then it is best that you practice your EYEROBICS and read each blend FIRST.

jump land   Ben and Gus jump on land.

just tent   Gus is just as fat as a big tent.

jogs pants   Ben jogs and Gus pants.

-mp

ca	cam	camp
du	dum	dump
ro	rom	romp
li	lim	limp
ju	jum	jump

-nd

fe	fen	fend
ha	han	hand
re	ren	rend
be	ben	bend
me	men	mend

-st

ru	rus	rust
be	bes	best
mi	mis	mist
la	las	last
ju	jus	just

-ft

le	lef	left
ra	raf	raft
li	lif	lift
tu	tuf	tuft
gi	gif	gift

COOPERATION is spelled with TWO LETTERS: "W" and "E"!

Ben	left	Ben left Gus on his raft.
just	lump	Gus is just a big, fat lump!
ants	milk	Ben fed Gus ham, jam, ants, figs, gum, and milk.

-nt

de	den	dent
re	ren	rent
mi	min	mint
ra	ran	rant
le	len	lent

-lk

si	sil	silk
mi	mil	milk
hu	hul	hulk
bu	bul	bulk
bi	bil	bilk

-lt

fe	fel	felt
be	bel	belt
me	mel	melt
hi	hil	hilt

-ld

gi	gil	gild
we	wel	weld
he	hel	held
me	mel	meld

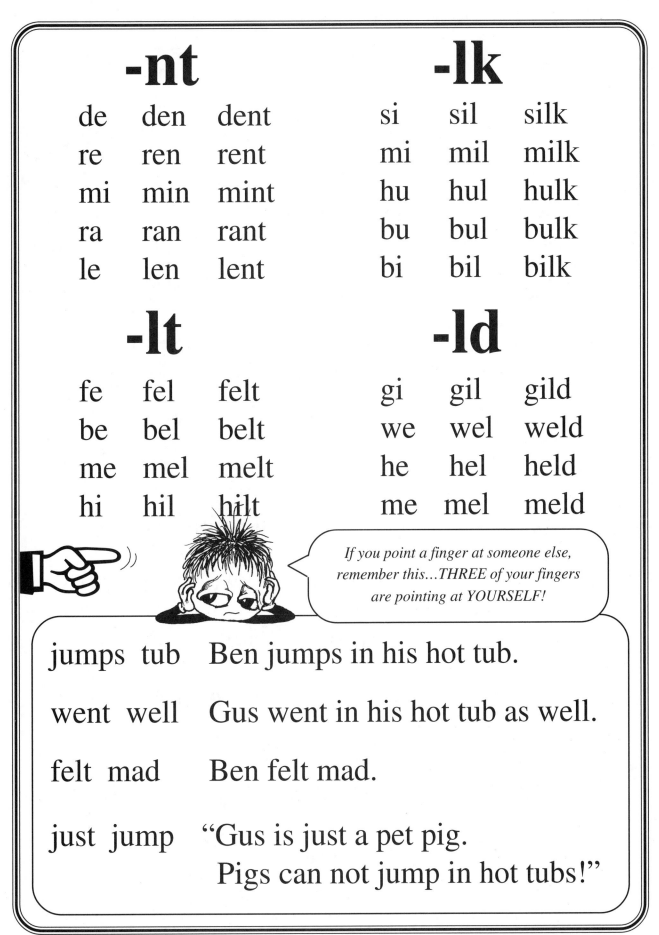

If you point a finger at someone else, remember this…THREE of your fingers are pointing at YOURSELF!

jumps tub	Ben jumps in his hot tub.
went well	Gus went in his hot tub as well.
felt mad	Ben felt mad.
just jump	"Gus is just a pet pig. Pigs can not jump in hot tubs!"

-lf

el   elf
gul   gulf
sel   self

-lp

hel   help
gul   gulp
kel   kelp

-pt

kep   kept
rap   rapt
wep   wept
kep   kept

-sk

cas   cask
tas   task
bas   bask
tus   tusk

-sp

lis   lisp
gas   gasp
ras   rasp
wis   wisp

red bug	A big, red bug bit Gus.
tusks hump	It had big tusks and a hump.
wept help	Gus wept, "Help! Help!"
leg bump	His leg had a big, bad bump on it.
limp lump	Gus fell in a big, limp lump.
must rest	Gus must rest. His bump must mend.

Read across the page:

rom romp	jum jump	pan pant
min mint	san sand	ben bend
run runt	hin hint	mil milk
res rest	hel help	rus rust
dam damp	gul gulp	san sand
sul sulk	fel felt	len lend
hel held	tas task	sel self
sen send	mis mist	

You can't climb the ladder of SUCCESS with your HANDS in your POCKETS!

held mints	Gus held ten big mints in his hand.
romps jumps	Gus romps and jumps on hot sand.
bends damp	Gus bends and gets a damp rock.
mints sand	His big mints fell on hot sand.
gulps mints	Gus gulps ten big sand mints!
felt sulks	Gus felt sick. Gus sulks a lot.

Read down each group first, then read across.

(Ugh—word lists can be daunting! Try reading just part of the page at a time, or to make it even more interesting use these words with some of the Hot Tips and Games beginning on page 250. It really makes things easier, and so much more fun besides!)

damp	mint	silk	lift	sent
ramp	hint	milk	sift	bent
camp	lint	bilk	gift	lent
lamp	tint		rift	dent
		bond		went
help	rest	pond	mask	rent
yelp	test	fond	task	tent
kelp	best		cask	
	vest	band		wept
felt	west	hand	pump	kept
belt	lest	land	lump	
pelt	nest	sand	bump	bust
welt	pest		jump	dust
melt		limp	dump	must
	send	wimp	hump	rust
fast	tend			just
mast	mend	runt	list	
past	lend	punt	fist	hilt
last	bend	hunt	mist	tilt
vast	fend			wilt
pant	weld	bulk	dusk	pulp
rant	held	sulk	tusk	gulp

TWO-CONSONANT ENDINGS REVIEW

Only the *beginning letter* is different in each of the following phrases:

went bent	sent lent	Kent sent
camp damp	lamp ramp	vamp camp
land sand	band hand	sand band
duck luck	buck suck	tuck muck
lump bump	dump jump	pump sump
fist list	mist fist	list mist
cask mask	bask task	ask mask

lift a gift

list in fist

rest is best

melt and felt

hunt his runt

yelp and help

hand in sand

These are phrases, not sentences. That's why they don't begin with a capital letter or end with a period.

dust and rust

duck has muck

jump on bump

bend and send

wept and kept

milk is silk

tusk at dusk

Once a day, read and then write the words on this page. Do this until you are able to read and spell them EASILY. You should be able to read these words WITHOUT having to sound out every letter. For example, if you find yourself reading "s-a-n-d" for "sand," cover up the last letter and read the three-letter blend first, "san-d," just as you did as instructed on page 56.

Continue reading words in this way until you are able to read them by blends and syllables automatically. (Eventually you will be able to read the whole word at a glance)

Reading sentences with mixed double-consonant endings can be difficult, and takes time. The Hot Tips and Games in the appendix can be of great assistance here. These activities and games will really reinforce and cement learning!

-y

A SUFFIX is an ending that is added to an existing word, which changes its use or meaning. In this section we shall learn the "-y" suffix.

Remember when we learned that there are five short-vowel sounds? There is *another* letter that is sometimes considered a vowel, also. It is the letter "y." When "y" is used as a suffix, it usually has a long "e" sound.

We simply add "y" to the end of a single-syllable word with a *double conso-nant* ending. The spelling of the root (or basic) word stays the *same*:

mist   mist-y   misty   misty

However, when "y" is added to the end of a single-syllable word which has only *one* consonant on the end, we must *double* that consonant before adding the "y" in order to keep the short-vowel sound:

fun   fun-n-y   funny   funny

Single-syllable, short-vowel words must *always* have a double consonant at the end before adding any suffixes beginning with a vowel. If the word does not end with a double consonant to begin with (as in "fun"), then we must double the last consonant before adding a suffix. If the word already ends with a double consonant (as in "mist"), we don't need to do this. Knowing these rules will really help your spelling!
Read these words once a day,
and then spell them
from dictation.

There is no secret of success except

HARD WORK!

There is only ONE PLACE where SUCCESS comes before WORK... Can you guess where?

In the DICTIONARY!

Here "y" is added to words with *two-consonant* endings.

Be sure your MIND is running before you put your MOUTH in gear!

and	And-y	Andy
dust	dust-y	dusty
hand	hand-y	handy
rust	rust-y	rusty
sand	sand-y	sandy
milk	milk-y	milky

dusty and rusty	jumpy and bumpy
handy and dandy	candy is sandy
silky and milky	lumpy and dumpy
Andy is sandy	husky and dusky
ducky and lucky	dolly is jolly
hulky and bulky	pesty and testy

jumpy sick	Ben felt jumpy and sick.
pesty bug	Ben has a pesty bug.
bumpy bed	Ben rests on his bumpy bed.
Gus hid	Gus hid in Ben's bed.
lumpy bump	Gus is a fat, lumpy bump in Ben's bed!

On this page, "y" is added to three-letter words with only *one* consonant at the end, and so we must *double* this consonant to keep the short-vowel sound:

run	run-n-y	runny
pen	pen-n-y	penny
sun	sun-n-y	sunny
Dan	Dan-n-y	Danny
fun	fun-n-y	funny
bun	bun-n-y	bunny

SEVEN DAYS without LAUGHTER MAKE ONE WEAK!

More three-word phrases to practice!

kitty is bitty	bunny is funny
Buzzy is fuzzy	Paddy has daddy
Jenny has penny	Buddy is muddy
sunny and runny	Danny has nanny
Bobby has hobby	puppy and guppy
Kenny and Benny	Kimmy and Jimmy

Jimmy fuzzy	Jimmy has a fuzzy bunny.
bunny Sammy	Jimmy's bunny is Sammy.
misty pond	Fuzzy Sammy fell in a misty pond.
funny muddy	Funny Sammy is muddy and wet!

These phrases are more difficult because they do not rhyme:

milky candy	silly Danny
rusty dolly	jazzy Sammy
sandy bunny	funny Penny
fuzzy kitty	dusty Bobby
muddy puppy	lucky Kenny
funny nanny	peppy Buddy

misty pond	I fell in a misty pond.
funny muddy	Gus is funny and muddy.
Jenny penny	Jenny has a rusty penny.
Andy fuzzy	Andy has a fuzzy kitty.
dusty windy	It is dusty and windy.
lumpy rock	His bed is lumpy.
	His bed is as lumpy as a big rock!

Review as many words as you can once a day. Read them first, and then write them.
Do this until you are able to read them SMOOTHLY and write them CORRECTLY...
... and just keep on going! Try to be like a DUCK...
It's calm on the SURFACE, but it paddles like mad UNDERNEATH!

TWIN-CONSONANT ENDINGS

Here's a *neat trick* to remember that will *really help* your *spelling!* When a short vowel in a one-syllable word is followed by a final "l," "f," "s," or "z," we usually *double* the letters in order to keep the short-vowel sound. Read across the page:

tell	fell	well	sell
will	hill	fill	dill
doll	loll	bell	dell

We LOSE GROUND when we SLING MUD...

Biff	jiff	tiff	miff
buff	puff	huff	muff

bass	Cass	lass	mass
sass	Bess	mess	Tess
hiss	kiss	miss	fuss

jazz	buzz	fuzz	fizz

tell Bess	sell Puff	kiss Tess
mass mess	fell well	will tell
Jess huff	fizz hiss	puff hill
mass mess	buff doll	lass tiff
miss Puff	Cass will	Jeff fell
Bess fuss	bass jazz	sell doll

FLUENCY REALITY CHECK
REAL AND NONSENSE WORDS

Why on earth would *anyone* want to spend time reading nonsense words? It turns out that many children who were taught phonics have incredible sight memories and unconsciously memorize words once they are shown how to decode them, frequently resulting in phonics skills falling by the wayside. And it certainly doesn't do a *thing* for spelling!

Reading nonsense words is an excellent way to check whether or not phonics skills are truly embedded in your learner's strategy when reading. They should be able to read both real and nonsense words with approximately the same degree of ease, accuracy, and speed. If they cannot, consider it a wake-up call!

Below is a list of nonsense words to use as a test of phonics skills learned so far. Have your student read about ten of these words out loud, and then choose ten words from any previous lesson, such as those on page 66. Each group of words should be read with approximately the same ease, speed, and accuracy.

If there is a large discrepancy between the two, it might be wise to include nonsense words in these lessons for a few minutes each day, or to go back to a particular phonics lesson that might be needed:

tas	boj	nes	pab	jid
waf	yut	gis	vem	foj
yim	pez	laj	kun	gox
heb	yaf	ses	mav	wep
ruck	pund	rab	pid	seffy
gond	belky	baft	semp	tast
rulp	hilf	vuz	tusty	jund
bock	kest	leck	ralk	rond
fosty	juck	himp	zendy	zeck

Now we are ready for something called CONSONANT DIGRAPHS.

So far, when we have had two consonants in a row, we have sounded out *each one*, as in "help." Both the "l" and the "p" are read.

Sometimes, two consonants next to each other make only *one* sound, that is different from *either one*.

Example: "sh" (We say *"shhhhhh"* when we want someone to be quiet.)

ru-sh rush   ba-sh bash   me-sh mesh

This kind of letter combination is known as a *consonant digraph*. In this section, we shall practice reading these digraphs at the *end* of words.(Every so often, just for fun, there is a "sneak preview" of what these digraphs sound like when put at the *beginning* of a word. More on beginnings later.)

T E A C H I N G   T I P: When reading the words in these lessons, keep a list of the ones that are especially difficult. There are always a few! After you have read the whole group of words, go back to the difficult ones and read them again, carefully. Be sure to include them in your spelling as well— writing them out will actually help make them *easier to read!*

Some of you may not be quite ready to read the sentences in these lessons. Or perhaps you are able to read them, but it is difficult. Unless you are able to read them fairly easily, here is a suggestion on how to proceed:

1. Read the two words to the left of the sentence. Have your teacher read the sentence to you while you move a finger slowly across the sentence, underneath each word. Follow her reading with your eyes, and when your teacher gets to each one of the two words you have just read, she will stop and let you read these words to her.

2. You and your teacher both read the same sentence TOGETHER.

3. Now you read the sentence YOURSELF! (If you are able to, that is. If not, only do steps one and two for a while—or even just step one.) Proceed in this manner for as many sentences in this book as you need to.

After you read a sentence, think about what happened. Can you describe it in your own words? Try doing this with a few practice sentences on every page from now on, to be sure that you understand what you are reading. Your teacher can tell you the meaning of any words that you may not know.

-sh

ba-sh	bash	ra-sh	rash
ma-sh	mash	sa-sh	sash
da-sh	dash	ga-sh	gash
ha-sh	hash	la-sh	lash
fi-sh	fish	di-sh	dish
wi-sh	wish	gu-sh	gush
hu-sh	hush	ru-sh	rush
ca-sh	cash	po-sh	posh

(sneak preview) sh-ip ship   sh-op shop

dash cash	posh shop	rash gash
mash bash	fish dish	gush lush
lash sash	hush mush	wish fish
rush cash	fish hash	bash mash
fish rush	ship cash	lash ship

*To ease ANOTHER'S heartache
is to forget one's OWN!*

dash cash	Let us dash and get cash. Hush!
shop ship	We can rush and shop on a ship.
wish fish	I wish I had a dish of fish hash.

-th

pa-th	path	wi-th	with
ba-th	bath	ma-th	math
ha-th	hath	pi-th	pith
Se-th	Seth	Be-th	Beth

(sneak preview) th-in thin th-ump thump

path bath	with Seth
hath math	path thin
thin path	Beth thump
with math	bath Beth

When your TEMPER gets the BEST of you it reveals the WORST in you!

Seth bath	Seth has a fish in his bath!
Beth math	Beth has a big math test.
Beth with	Beth runs with Jenny.
thin path	Beth runs with Jenny on a thin path.
thumps thin	Gus thumps a thin, red bug.

thin fish	with cash	dash shop
Beth wish	posh bath	Beth math
dash path	Seth wish	rush path
math ship	thump bug	bath gush
with hash	rush hush	fish mushy

fish mushy	His fish is mushy.
posh bath	Seth has a posh bath!
with math	Dad helps with math.
thin fish	Gus has a thin fish.
dash path	I dash with Jan up a path.
Seth wish	Seth has a wish.
rush path	Let us rush on a path.
wish Beth	I wish Beth had cash.

Review as many of these words as you can, once a day.
  Read them first, and then write them from dictation.
Continue doing this with every lesson in the book.
  Take all the time you need. There is no hurry!
You are NOT running a race…
  …you are learning how to READ!
And be SURE to check out the great games, activities,
  and tips beginning on page 250!
(The spelling guide on page 238 is also extremely helpful
  if you are seriously teaching spelling at this point.)

-ch, -tch

This digraph is usually spelled "ch" if it follows a *consonant:*

pun-ch	punch	lun-ch	lunch
ran-ch	ranch	bun-ch	bunch
pin-ch	pinch	ben-ch	bench

When this digraph follows a *vowel*, it is usually spelled "tch":

pi-tch	pitch	fe-tch	fetch
ca-tch	catch	re-tch	retch
no-tch	notch	ma-tch	match
la-tch	latch	pa-tch	patch

Exceptions to this rule are: rich such much

Take it easy with these "-ch" and "-tch" words, and read across the page:

much lunch	such lunch	rich lunch
ranch lunch	hunch lunch	lunch bunch
catch latch	fetch latch	hitch latch
pitch match	catch match	fetch match
Dutch hutch	patch hutch	latch hutch

GOOD JUDGMENT comes from GOOD EXPERIENCE...
And GOOD EXPERIENCE comes from BAD JUDGMENT!

Mitch pinch   Mitch can pinch and punch!

match catch   Can Ben match his fish catch?

fetch lunch   Mitch will fetch such a big lunch!

hunch Dutch   He has a hunch Pat is Dutch.

pitch catch   Mom can pitch and catch well.

catch fetch   Catch his cat and fetch it lunch.

fetch punch   Fetch Gus lunch and punch.

match bench   A match fell on his bench.

catch ditch   His cats catch rats in a ditch.

munch lunch   Gus and Ben munch such a rich lunch!

There's a lot of FREE CHEESE in mousetraps, But you'll never find any HAPPY MICE there...

Hmmmmmmm......?

Let's review the consonant digraph and two-consonant endings together. Read down first—all of the words in each column have the same *endings*. Now read across—all of the words have the same *beginnings*, but different *endings!* Take all the time you need to read and write these words easily:

mash	math	match	mask	Mack
bash	bath	batch	bask	back
wish	with			wick
	path	patch		pack
hash	hath	hatch		hack
dish		ditch	disk	Dick
mush		much	musk	muck
		Dutch	dusk	duck
hush		hutch	husk	
cash		catch	cask	

A WINNER says, "LET'S FIND OUT!"
A LOSER says, "NOBODY KNOWS!"

-ck	Jack is back	peck on deck
-sk	risk a disk	mask in cask
-sh	fish in dish	hush and rush
-th	Beth and Seth	math in bath
-ch	rich is much	such a lunch
-tch	hutch is Dutch	Mitch has itch

These phrases have mixed words, and may be difficult to read. *Take your time!*

bug is fuzzy	candy is best
test is funny	Pat has math
Beth has hunch	camp is sunny
pinch and itch	penny is cash
latch on rack	shop on ship
fetch a dish	jelly in lunch
Mitch is thin	kitty is silky
Gus is fussy	catch big fish
dash in wind	jog and jump
pack his sack	path is thin
Rick is sick	such bad luck
his buddy Jack	cat can catch
Andy is silly	catch his pitch
ditch is sandy	Jenny has milk

Some people are like
WHEELBARROWS...
They work only when PUSHED,
And are very easily UPSET!

-ing

s-ing	sing		r-ing	ring
p-ing	ping		w-ing	wing
k-ing	king		b-ing	bing
d-ing	ding		l-ing	ling

(sneak preview) th-ing thing

-ang

r-ang	rang		h-ang	hang
b-ang	bang		f-ang	fang
g-ang	gang		s-ang	sang

-ung

r-ung	rung		s-ung	sung
h-ung	hung		m-ung	mung

-ong

s-ong	song		d-ong	dong
l-ong	long		p-ong	pong
g-ong	gong		t-ong	tong

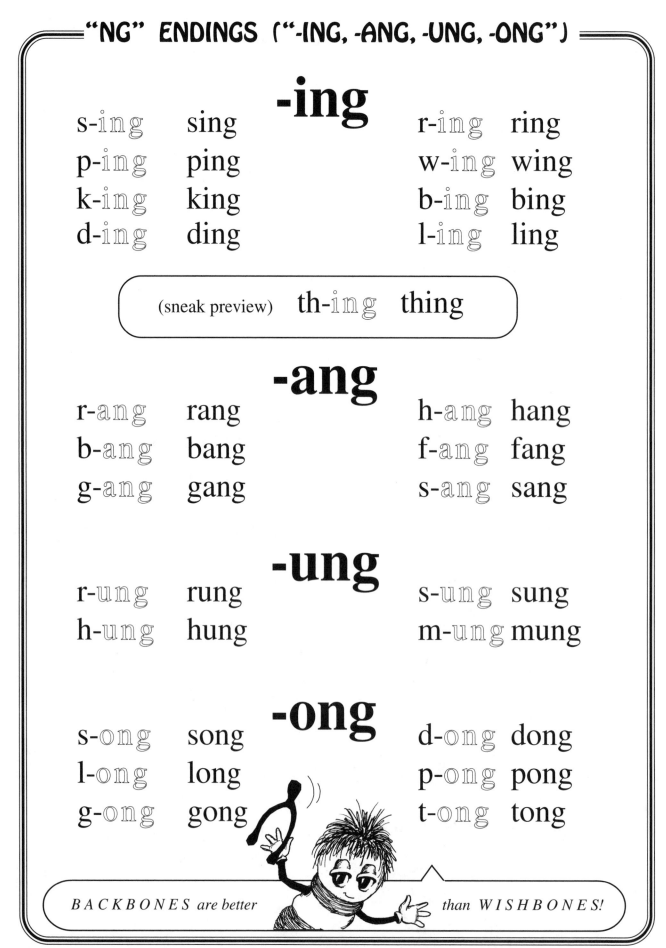

B A C K B O N E S are better ... *than W I S H B O N E S!*

Read across the page:

sing	sang	song	sung
Bing	bang	dong	dung
king	kong	bing	bong
long	ring	fang	hung

sing song	ding dong	King Kong
gang sang	hung rung	long song
ping pong	king sung	wing fang

EVERYONE who got where he IS, FIRST started out from where he WAS!

ping pong	Ping pong is fun.
king sing	A king can sing well.
rung hung	I hung on a long rung.
tongs hung	His tongs hung on a rung.
King Kong	King Kong had long fangs.
gang wings	A bat gang has long wings.
rang sang	I rang and I sang a long song.
Bing sang	Bing sang "Ding, Dong, Dell."

fish-ing	fishing	help-ing	helping
wish-ing	wishing	dash-ing	dashing
bash-ing	bashing	limp-ing	limping
gasp-ing	gasping	jump-ing	jumping
bend-ing	bending	send-ing	sending
sing-ing	singing	rush-ing	rushing

patching matching	ringing singing
packing sacking	helping yelping
sending bending	itching ditching
jumping bumping	dashing bashing

The GREATEST MISTAKE you can MAKE in life is to be CONTINUALLY FEARING you will MAKE ONE!

Andy rushing	Andy is rushing and dashing.
Ben helping	Ben is helping and packing.
Jan jumping	Jan is jumping and itching.
Pat singing	Pat is singing and fishing.
Gus gulping	Gus is gulping and munching a big, fat fish lunch!

-ink

s-ink	sink	p-ink	pink
l-ink	link	k-ink	kink
r-ink	rink	w-ink	wink
f-ink	fink	m-ink	mink

(sneak preview) th-ink think

-ank

s-ank	sank	b-ank	bank
d-ank	dank	H-ank	Hank
r-ank	rank	t-ank	tank
y-ank	yank	l-ank	lank

(sneak preview) th-ank thank

-unk

s-unk	sunk	b-unk	bunk
d-unk	dunk	l-unk	lunk
h-unk	hunk	j-unk	junk
p-unk	punk	g-unk	gunk

(sneak preview) ch-unk chunk

If OBSTACLES get in your way, do as the WIND does... WHISTLE and go AROUND THEM!

Read across the page:

ink	sink	sinking		ink	link	linking
ank	bank	banking		ank	yank	yanking
unk	dunk	dunking		unk	bunk	bunking
ink	link	linking		ink	sink	sinking
ank	yank	yanking		ank	rank	ranking
unk	bunk	bunking		unk	junk	junking
ink	wink	winking		ink	kink	kinking

Read and write each of these words from dictation…and then move on.

Just keep on going! Keep this in mind:
ALL progress involves SOME risk…
…You can't steal SECOND BASE
and keep your FOOT on FIRST!

Hank sinking	Hank is sinking fast!
pink bunk	Hank has a pink bunk.
tank sank	His tank sank in a pond.
winking Hank	Jan is winking at Hank!
hunk dunking	He is dunking a hunk of ham in his pink sink.

Up to this point, we have been building words using only short-vowel sounds. Now we are ready to learn some other vowel sounds.

In this section, we shall learn the *long* sound of each vowel. In a way, these are easiest to learn of all, because the long sound of each vowel is simply its *own name!*

The diacritical mark for a long-vowel sound is a straight line over the top of the vowel, like this:

$$A\bar{a} \quad E\bar{e} \quad I\bar{i} \quad O\bar{o} \quad U\bar{u}$$

The way we most frequently make a word with a long vowel sound in it is to add the letter "e" to the end of a three-letter word. The "e" we have added stays silent, but it changes the *short* vowel sound in the word to a *long* vowel sound. It is often called the "MAGIC E." Here is how it works:

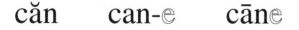

$$c\breve{a}n \qquad can\text{-}e \qquad c\bar{a}ne$$

The long-vowel diacritical mark is called a "macron," and the short-vowel diacritical mark is called a "breve." Strange but interesting names!

We shall spend the next several pages reading words with long-vowel sounds. As always, read the words first, then spell them from dictation. You probably know to do this by now without being reminded! Therefore, from now on we will not say it very often. Please remember to *read* and then *write* the words in *EACH LESSON FOR THE REST OF THIS BOOK!*

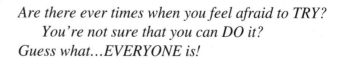

Are there ever times when you feel afraid to TRY?
  You're not sure that you can DO it?
Guess what...EVERYONE is!

It's ALL RIGHT to be afraid...it's only necessary that
  your courage be just a LITTLE BIT BIGGER
  than your fear.

Courage is RESISTANCE to fear and OVERCOMING it.
  It is NEVER LACK of fear.

Aā

Read down each set of words (can, cane, etc.). If it is *too difficult* to keep switching from short-vowel sounds to long-vowel sounds, try reading *across* each row first: all the short-vowel words together, then the long-vowel words. Then try reading down each set *again,* and see if it is a little easier this time.

căn	hăt	căp	măd
cāne	hāte	cāpe	māde
pan	fat	tap	gap
pane	fate	tape	gape
Sam	fad	bass	man
same	fade	base	mane
Dan	Jan	bad	ban
Dane	Jane	bade	bane

Notice how the "ck" endings change to just "k" when "e" is added:

tack	Mack	back	lack
take	make	bake	lake
Jack	rack	sack	tack
Jake	rake	sake	take

Don't always FOLLOW where a path may lead…
Sometimes go where there IS no path, and leave a TRAIL for OTHERS to follow!

LONG "A" REVIEW

These words all have a long "a" sound. Read across the page:

bake cake	Jake rake	safe gate
late date	take game	same lake
made cape	rate Jane	mate wave
name tape	ate cake	fake pane

These words combine the long "a" sound with lessons previously learned:

best sale	fish sale	duck sale
lock gate	ranch gate	cat gate
wish cake	rich cake	pink cake
bass lake	muddy lake	misty lake
fussy Jake	catch Jake	pinch Jake

Jane made	Jane and Jake made a date cake.
ate safe	Gus ate his cake at a safe lake.
Jake lake	Jake fell in a muddy, pale lake.
take fake	Take his fake cat and name it.
makes tapes	Jane makes tapes, canes and rakes.

Happiness does not come from what you HAVE…
it comes from what you ARE!

Ii

(Proceed as with long "a" for this page and the rest of the long vowels.)

rĭp	hĭd	dĭn	rĭd
rīpe	hīde	dīne	rīde
kit	pin	win	dim
kite	pine	wine	dime
bit	pill	fill	mill
bite	pile	file	mile
lick	pick	Dick	hick
like	pike	dike	hike

PEOPLE are like TEA BAGS...
They don't know their own STRENGTH
until they're in HOT WATER!

These words all have a long "i" sound. Read across:

dīve tīde	wīde sīze	līfe mīne
wine vine	pile tile	wife hike
bite lime	five limes	wire tire
hide pipe	fine dime	nine dimes
live hive	Mike files	dine time

These words combine the long "i" sound with lessons previously learned. Read across the page:

bug bite	cat bite	duck bite
ride bike	take bike	with bike
dive tide	misty tide	pick tide
fine limes	bumpy limes	suck limes
mile hike	Jack hike	sang hike
live vine	yank vine	pinch vine
pile fish	pile sand	pile lunch
song time	dunking time	funny time
like Rick	like Hank	like jumping

time hike	It is time to hike five miles.
hide five	Hide his five dimes on his bike.
Mike ride	Mike will ride a wide tire.
wife fine	His wife likes a fine hike.
likes bite	Gus likes to bite five limes.

To treat your FACTS with IMAGINATION is ONE THING...

But to IMAGINE your FACTS is ANOTHER!

Ō ō

hŏp	cŏp	mŏp	rŏb
hōpe	cōpe	mŏpe	rōbe

tot	not	cod	rod
tote	note	code	rode

doll	lop	pock	jock
dole	lope	poke	joke

SMILES

Do you know what the LONGEST WORD in the English language REALLY IS?
It is "SMILES." Can you guess WHY?   (The answer is upside down.)

Answer: because there is a "MILE" between the first and last letters!

These words all have a long "o" sound:

rode home	lone sole	mole hole
woke doze	hope rode	mope home
moles rove	note robe	woke joke
hope dome	hole rope	lope pole
tote bone	note vote	rove home
hope joke	poke robe	cope code

Whenever you find yourself working TOO HARD over the SAME KIND of sound, go back and review that lesson. It is EXPECTED that this will happen from time to time. Some lessons need more reinforcement than others—and EACH PERSON IS DIFFERENT.

Reviewing what you have already learned is not only the BEST way to be sure you really know it well, it is the ONLY way!

These words combine the long "o" sound with lessons previously learned. Read across the page:

big rope	patch rope	hang rope
neck bone	yank bone	such bone
pink robe	long robe	fetch robe
poke bug	poke Jack	poke Hank
rode fast	rode wave	rode raft
made joke	big joke	nine jokes
Kate hoping	Jean hoping	Mike hoping

mole pokes	A mole pokes holes in his home.
notes robe	Jill notes Jan's long, pink robe.
woke rode	Mike woke up and rode home.
tote bone	Tote a long bone on a bulky rope.
woke mopes	Gus woke. He mopes in his robe.

There are *two ways* to say the long "u" sound, with a *slightly different* diacritical mark for each one:

These words say "yoo:" # Uū=yoo

| cŭt | mŭtt | ŭs | cŭb |
| cūte | mūte | ūse | cūbe |

| cute mule | use mule | cure mule |
| pure mute | cure cube | use cube |

These words say "oo:" # Uū=oo

| tub | luck | duck | rub |
| tube | Luke | duke | Rube |

| rude June | rule Luke | tune lute |
| Luke duke | June rule | tube tune |

Try to do something every day, even if you're feeling LOW and only do a LITTLE BIT...
Be like the SUN... it has a SINKING SPELL every night, but still comes back up SHINING
EVERY MORNING!

LONG "U" REVIEW

These words contain *both* long "u" sounds. When you *say* the word, you will *soon see which* sound *fits best!* Read across the page:

cute June	pure tune	rude mule
use tube	mute rule	cure June
pure cube	cute duke	duke lute
use lute	June mute	rude duke
cure Luke	duke use	cute mule
use tube	cute tunes	June rude

He who KICKS CONTINUOUSLY SOON LOSES his BALANCE!

use June	Use June Lake; it is pure.
tune cute	I tune a cute red van.
June tunes	June and Luke sing tunes.
duke rules	A rude duke rules back home.
use mules	We use mules to hike up bumpy hills.
Luke uses	Luke uses pure cubes in his cup.

Guess what? There are *several* ways to spell the long "e" sound besides just adding an "e" to the end of a short-vowel word. In this section we shall learn the "ee" and "ea" spellings of this sound as well as the "magic e":

pĕt	tĕn	bĕd
Pēte	tēēn	bē̆ad

("Ee" and "ea" are actually vowel digraphs: two letters with only one sound. We shall have more vowel digraphs later.)

ē=e–e

here	Eve	Pete

Read across:

ē=ee

see	seek	seen	seed
fee	feet	feed	feel
wee	weep	weed	week
bee	beet	beef	beep
Dee	deed	deep	peep
heed	heel	peek	peel

SOMETHING TO THINK ABOUT: From now on, there will often be more than one way to spell a sound, with no rules to go by at all! So you can see how it would be difficult to learn how to SPELL these kinds of words at the same time that you are learning how to READ them!

In order to learn how to read as quickly as possible, it might be best to have each spelling group dictated SEPARATELY, by "family," when you write these words; and then move on to the next lesson.

Later on, you can always come back to these sections for more detailed spelling lessons. It's also true that much spelling is simply "picked up" along the way, by simply reading books.

(When you do decide to teach spelling, be SURE to check out "Spelling Strategies" on page 238. It is a step-by-step guide on how to teach spelling with this book.)

ē=ea Read down each group:

sea	**ea**	**tea**
sea	eat	tea
seat	east	team
seam	each	teach

bea	**lea**	**rea**
beat	leaf	read
bead	lead	real
beak	leap	rear
beam	leak	reap
beach	leach	reach

There are THREE KINDS of people in this world…
1–those who MAKE things happen,
2–those who WATCH things happen,
3–and those who WONDER what's happening!

ear hear	heel feet	peep cheep
team teach	see bead	deep peal
seek peak	weak weed	gear here
near Dee	real peach	beast beak
reach leak	each bee	east beach

When a two-letter word ends in "e," it has a long sound:

me   be   he   we   she

feed me	she leaps	we see
be seen	be here	she eats
we reach	he means	near me
eat beets	she feeds	he seeks
treating me	teaching me	be weak

These words combine the long "e" sound with lessons previously learned.
Take time to review any rules that are especially difficult. Read across:

be here	be home	be fast
see me	feed Nick	ring me
we treat	wake me	feed fish
lean beef	pure beef	rich beef
feed me	gulp treat	Dee leaps
kids leap	reach latch	reach bunk
sink beach	bunny leaps	misty beach
reach duck	fishing beach	gulping treats
teaching me	teaching math	teaching Jack

A ship in a harbor is SAFE...   ...but that's NOT what ships are BUILT FOR!

feed neat	We feed each neat cat beef.
she eating	She is seen eating real meat.
seek mean	We seek each mean bee on Dee.
each peals	Each bell peals near and clear.
leaps peak	He leaps on a peak near a beach.
weak peach	Feed me weak tea and a peach.
leaping each	See Pete leaping on each leaf.
Dee teaching	Dee is team teaching reading.
peeks beast	She peeks and sees a big beast.
leap each	See Gus leap and eat each bee!
weeds peaches	Gus is eating weeds, bees, peas, tea, beef, meat, and a big peach.

*JUST THINK of how FAR you have come!
Always compare yourself ONLY with the progress
YOU YOURSELF have made...
NEVER compare yourself with other people.
After all, if only the BEST BIRDS sang,
the WOODS would be SILENT!*

Read across:

cake sale	bake sale	bake cake
fake lake	name lake	fake name

a

see beast	beach beast	see beach
Pete read	teach read	Pete teach

e

wide dive	wife dive	wide wife
like Mike	bite Mike	like bite

i

mope home	mole home	mole mope
tote note	code note	tote code

o

cute June	rule June	cute rule
use tube	Luke tube	use Luke

u

use rake	neat joke	we dive
poke cake	hide me	we vote
team teach	beast leaps	pure lake
cute deer	fake tune	make cube
five seeds	deep lake	rake weeds
ripe peach	he reads	she leaps
take bite	bake meat	cute Kate

Phonics Pathways: Clear Steps to Easy Reading and Perfect Spelling

There is a group of words that has a long vowel sound, *without* having an "e" at the end. Many of the long "o" words end in "-ld," and long "i" words in "-nd." Practice reading and spelling them. Read across the page:

o

old	sold	told	gold
bold	bolt	cold	mold
hold	fold	colt	jolt
post	host	most	both
so	no	go	roll

i

find	rind	kind	mind
tiny	hind	wild	mild

Ideas are FUNNY THINGS...
THEY don't work unless YOU DO!

These words all have long-vowel sounds:

hide me	old pine	cold jolt
told Luke	so cold	find gold
no bite	roll dime	sold bike
we joke	mile toll	wild beast
so kind	both kites	mind Jane
fine mind	go home	tiny colt
fold cane	Mike host	find robe
teach colt	told Mike	hold peach
tiny beach	pile gold	both kinds

The words in these phrases combine long-vowel words without the "e" at the end with short-vowel words. Reading across, one word in each phrase is the same:

old socks	old fish	old song
mild mint	mild duck	mild lunch
so sick	so lucky	so much
sing most	catch most	kick most
wish gold	fetch gold	lend gold
wild kitty	wild hunch	wild dash
cold bath	cold bench	cold mist

HAPPINESS is like a BUTTERFLY…
The more you CHASE it,
The more it will ELUDE you…
But if you turn your attention to OTHER THINGS,
it comes and SOFTLY SITS on your SHOULDER!

go find   Go and find a cute, tiny old pine.

wild sold   A wild old man sold so much gold!

old cold   An old, cold lake is wild and deep.

kind mild   A kind, mild colt folds its tiny legs.

no both   No, both kids can go and find Jane.

find most   We find Luke most kind and bold.

Let's take time to practice reading short- and long-vowel words together. Take one group of phrases at a time. These words all contain the SAME VOWEL, but it is SHORT in the first word and LONG in the second. Read DOWN each column first: all of the short-vowel words, and then all of the long-vowel words. Now read these phrases ACROSS. (Reading short- and long-vowel words together may take more time!)

ă ā

băck	gāte	Dăn	dāte	făt	cāke
Sam	came	cat	lame	sad	fate
can	make	jam	fake	ham	bake
fan	game	cash	case	math	base
sad	Jake	dad	rake	ranch	lake
pack	tape	catch	Jane	map	sale
damp	cave	lamp	base	has	date

ĭ ī

fĭsh	bīte	Kĭt	hīde	sĭt	dīke
kid	Mike	with	life	hid	dime
pick	lime	big	hike	pig	hide
his	bike	win	kite	fit	pipe
in	time	wig	mine	tin	mine
lift	tire	Rick	bite	big	tide
is	fine	fin	wide	Nick	dine

ŏ   ō

lŏck	hōme	pŏp	bōne	gŏt	mōle
Don	rode	on	dome	mob	woke
top	pole	job	hope	mock	vote
not	code	rock	cone	hop	cove
pot	hole	Tod	poke	cop	joke
hot	note	Bob	doze	mop	home

ŭ   ū

hŭg	Lūke	pŭp	cūte	bŭg	mūte
gulp	cube	duck	rude	lucky	June
fun	Yule	tug	mule	sun	cure

ĕ   ē

wĕt	tēa	mĕt	mē	rĕd	mēat
well	deep	set	bean	ten	bees
Beth	keep	pet	seek	Meg	dear
fed	meal	led	jeep	leg	weak
beg	Dee	get	deer	Les	weep

The BROOK would lose its SONG if we REMOVED THE ROCKS!

she read	She can read as well as Jane.
Luke takes	Luke takes a rake and weeds.
bikes home	She bikes home five miles.
each cute	Each cute mole is peeking.
hopes time	Gus hopes it is time to eat.
five bees	Five bees hide in a safe hive.
Pete pokes	Pete pokes a hole in a dike.
bites pokes	Dee bites, pokes, and mopes.
June dive	See June dive in a deep lake!
hikes miles	He hikes five miles and takes Mike's fine mules.

Speak not SOUR words, but SWEET…
For someone may REPEAT 'em.
But EVEN WORSE, there MAY be times
When YOU will have to EAT 'EM!
(Crabs DIG and spiders BITE…
So do HURTFUL WORDS… RIGHT?)

On page 68 we learned that endings added to words are called "suffixes," and that when you add a "y" suffix to a short-vowel word with only *one* consonant at the end, you must *double* that consonant first to keep the short-vowel sound:

fun   fun-n-y   funny

We also learned you don't *have* to add an extra letter if the word *already ends* in two consonants:

mist   mist-y   misty

The *important thing to remember* is that short-vowel words must *always* end with a double consonant before adding *any* suffix beginning with a vowel. Let's try "ing" suffixes first. Read across the page:

-ing

sit   sit-t-ing   sitting
hop   hop-p-ing   hopping

hop-ping	hopping	run-ning	running
kid-ding	kidding	rot-ting	rotting
set-ting	setting	bug-ging	bugging
hug-ging	hugging	sip-ping	sipping
sun-ning	sunning	tan-ning	tanning
hit-ting	hitting	lag-ging	lagging
hum-ming	humming	tap-ping	tapping

Of all the things you WEAR, your EXPRESSION is the most important!

nap	napping	kid	kidding
hop	hopping	get	getting
jog	jogging	pat	patting
let	letting	pet	petting
hug	hugging	hit	hitting
run	running	hum	humming
win	winning	sip	sipping
tug	tugging	sit	sitting

running and humming

hopping and popping

tugging and bugging

bidding and kidding

bagging and sagging

PEOPLE are much like FISH... NEITHER would get into trouble if they kept their MOUTHS SHUT!

Mom is humming and singing a hit tune.

Gus is panting and jogging up a big hill.

Jack is sitting and sipping his mint tea.

Jan is lifting and tugging a wet fish.

I am kidding and bugging my fat cat.

The "-ed" suffixes can be pronounced in *three different ways:*

ed=-ed
(It is always pronounced "ed" if a word ends in "d" or "t:")

melt melted	end ended	rent rented
lift lifted	wind winded	land landed

d=-ed

nag nagged	hum hummed	pin pinned
jam jammed	tag tagged	rob robbed

t=-ed

jump jumped	mop mopped	hop hopped
kiss kissed	back backed	kick kicked

People are a lot like CARS...
Some are best racing UP a hill,
Others work best going DOWN a hill...
And when you hear one KNOCKING all the time,
It's a sure sign that something's wrong under the HOOD!

pin pinned	tap tapped	lift lifted
rent rented	bag bagged	rip ripped
nag nagged	cap capped	tug tugged
dim dimmed	jam jammed	sob sobbed

rented and dented	lifted and sifted
nagged and bagged	bugged and tugged
hopped and popped	sipped and dipped

Here are some "-er" suffixes: **-er**

hug hugger	kid kidder	win winner
set setter	tan tanner	wet wetter
sip sipper	big bigger	jog jogger
run runner	hot hotter	nag nagger

jogger is wetter	runner is tanner
tipper is bigger	winner is better
nagger is hotter	mopper is sadder

SHORT-VOWEL ENDINGS REVIEW

Short-vowel words with *double-consonant* endings: (Ending *already* doubled!)

kick	kicked	kicking	kicker
pack	packed	packing	packer
kiss	kissed	kissing	kisser
rent	rented	renting	renter
jump	jumped	jumping	jumper

Short-vowel words with *single-consonant* endings: (Must double ending *first!*)

mop	mopped	mopping	mopper
rob	robbed	robbing	robber
tug	tugged	tugging	tugger
pet	petted	petting	petter
tip	tipped	tipping	tipper

Something INTERESTING happens when we add these suffixes to long-vowel "magic e" words. (These words, as you have already learned, end in silent "e.") First we drop the silent "e," and then we add the suffix:

bike = bik~~e~~ + ing = bik-ing = biking

bike = bik~~e~~ + ed = bik-ed = biked

bike = bik~~e~~ + er = bik-er = biker

We do *not* double the last consonant of the word because we need a *single-consonant ending* in order to keep the long-vowel sound:

poke	poking	poked	poker
doze	dozing	dozed	dozer
save	saving	saved	saver
rake	raking	raked	raker

The words in each of these phrases have the *same* long vowel:

baking and raking	baker raked
voting and hoping	voter hoped
taking and naming	taker named
joking and poking	joker poked

The words in *these* phrases each have *different* long vowels:

dining and saving	diner saved
raking and leaping	raker leaped
moping and hating	moper hated
riding and dozing	rider dozed

SUFFIX SPELLING CHART

Short-vowel words must always have *two* consonants before adding a suffix beginning with a vowel, to keep the short-vowel sound. *Long-vowel* words need only *one*. Each pair of short and long-vowel words listed below has almost the same spelling, except for double or single-consonant endings before the suffix. This changes the *meaning* of the word as well as its *pronunciation*. (Reminder: spell short-vowel words "-ck" if they end with a "k" sound.) Read across the page:

	LONG VOWEL	SHORT VOWEL	LONG VOWEL	SHORT VOWEL
	mōping	mŏpping	rāking	răcking
-ing	riding	ridding	baking	backing
	filing	filling	liking	licking
	hoping	hopping	taking	tacking
	taping	tapping	stoking	stocking
-ed	pined	pinned	liked	licked
	taped	tapped	hoped	hopped
	baked	backed	moped	mopped
	poked	pocked	caned	canned
-er	diner	dinner	baker	backer
	hoper	hopper	taker	tacker
	biker	bicker	taper	tapper
	filer	filler	moper	mopper

*People who brag about their ancestors are like CARROTS...
the BEST PART of them is UNDERGROUND!*

111

hoping diver   We are hoping to see a diver.

jogging runner A jogging runner kicked a can.

baker liked   His baker liked baking cakes.

saved tasting   We saved lunch, tasting just a bit.

joker kidding   See the joker kidding and poking.

raked saved   Jan raked and saved five dimes.

landed backed   A jet landed fast and backed up.

hissed robber   Kitty hissed and bit the robber!

jogged napped   He jogged fast and then napped.

baked licked   Gus baked, licked, gulped, and
                 munched candy. He felt sick!

*Diamonds cannot be polished
without a lot of
RUBBING and FRICTION...
And PEOPLE cannot be PERFECTED
without a lot of
TRIALS and CHALLENGES!*

SYLLABLES are small parts into which long words can be divided. Each syllable contains *one* vowel sound, and *that's* how you can tell how many syllables there are in a word! When we divide long words into syllables, we *hyphenate* them—that is, we put a dash between each syllable. We *accent* the syllable which gets the most emphasis when read by putting a slanted line after it. The longest word in the world is easily read once it is broken up into syllables! First, read each syllable below:

Now read these syllables in a DIFFERENT ORDER, and see what happens. *(It is something that YOU are for having come SO FAR in this book!)*

Fan-tas´-tic!

lim´-it limit	ex´-it exit
vis´-it visit	un-til´ until
tid´-bit tidbit	tab´-let tablet
rob´-in robin	wag´-on wagon
cab´-in cabin	sub-mit´ submit
rab´-bit rabbit	pig´-pen pigpen
pen´-cil pencil	him-self´ himself
in-tend´ intend	cab´-i-net cabinet

Here is the longest word in the dictionary! Count the number of vowels, and then count the number of syllables. Are these numbers both the same?

an´-ti-dis´-es-tab´-lish-men-tar´-i-an-ism´

We have learned that the "k" sound at the end of single-syllable short-vowel words is spelled "-ck." However, the "k" sound at the end of *multisyllable* short-vowel words is spelled with a "-c." Read across the page:

k=-ic

col´-ic colic   frol´-ic frolic

ton´-ic tonic   son´-ic sonic

fran´-tic frantic   pan´-ic panic

man´-ic manic   an´-tic antic

tar´-mac tarmac   com´-ic comic

fan-tas´-tic fantastic ter-rif´-ic terrific

Whew…

When a suffix beginning with a vowel is added to these words, the "-c" ending is changed to "-ck." (Remember what we learned on page 51? "It's 'k' and not 'c' followed by 'i' or an 'e.'") Sigh…why is spelling SO COMPLICATED?

k =-ick

frol-ic	frol-ick-ed	frol-ick-ing
mim-ic	mim-ick-ed	mim-ick-ing
pic-nic	pic-nick-ed	pic-nick-ing
pan-ic	pan-ick-ed	pan-ick-ing

frol´-ic at pic´-nic   frolic at picnic

mim´-ic a com´-ic   mimic a comic

wit´-ness is fran´-tic   witness is frantic

Gus ate terrific, fantastic tidbits at his picnic!

Are there any special rules to use when we divide a word into syllables?
YES! Short-vowel words are divided *differently* from long-vowel words:

Short-vowel words are divided *after* the consonant. It is a *"closed"* division:

prof-it	cab-in	lim-it	him-self
ex-it	rob-in	wag-on	prod-uct

When the vowel is followed by two consonants, it is a short-vowel word and is hyphenated *between* the consonants:

rud-dy	fuz-zy	mop-ping	hol-ly
pop-py	mud-dy	hop-ping	pen-ny

Long-vowel words are hyphenated *before* the consonant. This is called an *"open"* division:

fu-ry	ru-by	Ka-ty	ho-ly
ra-ven	pro-gram	ha-zy	la-zy

Exception: A suffix added to a word is always kept together. For example, we do not write "po-king" with an open division, even though it has a long-vowel sound. We keep the "-ing" in a syllable by itself:

pok-ing	cur-ing	bik-ing	mop-ing
hop-ing	rid-ing	hid-ing	doz-ing
bik-er	rid-er	mak-er	bak-er

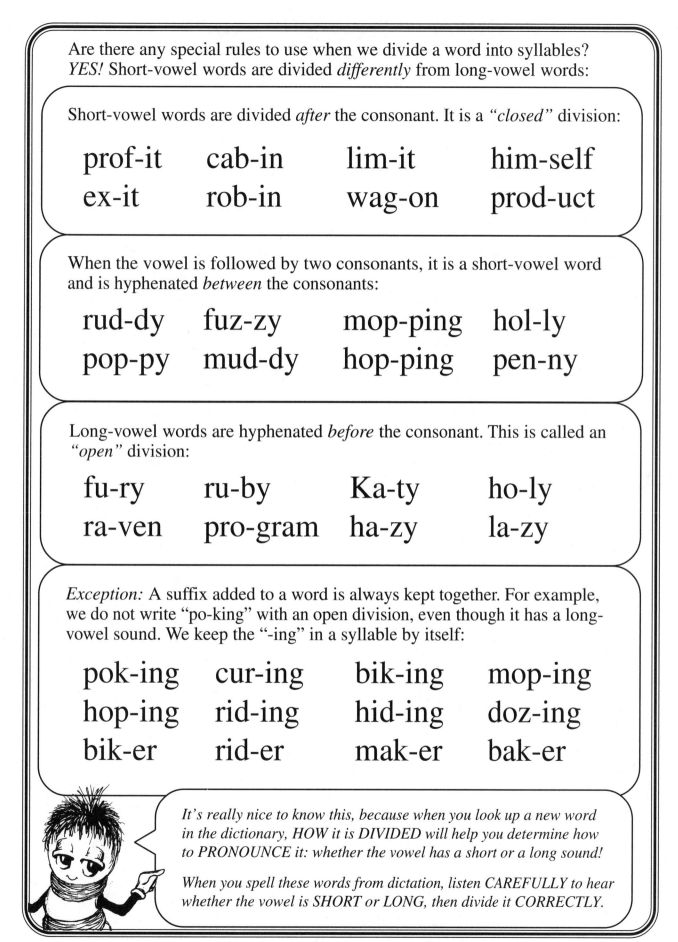

It's really nice to know this, because when you look up a new word in the dictionary, HOW it is DIVIDED will help you determine how to PRONOUNCE it: whether the vowel has a short or a long sound!

When you spell these words from dictation, listen CAREFULLY to hear whether the vowel is SHORT or LONG, then divide it CORRECTLY.

PLURAL, POSSESSIVE AND "X"

"Plural" means *more than one*. Most of the time we just add "s" to the word:

top	tops	duck	ducks
king	kings	cat	cats
peg	pegs	bug	bugs

With words ending in "sh," "ch," "tch," "z," and "s" (also "x," which we shall learn on the next page) the plural is formed by adding "es." (The "es" plurals actually sound more like "ez" when spoken!)

batch	batch-es	gush	gush-es
fish	fish-es	fizz	fizz-es
inch	inch-es	kiss	kiss-es

Don't point a FINGER... lend a HAND!

Read across the page:

cans	dishes	pans	matches
jugs	wishes	mugs	batches
kicks	bashes	licks	catches
tops	rushes	mops	fizzes
pegs	fishes	kegs	rings
racks	sacks	packs	backs
bells	quizzes	gushes	inches
kisses	catches	matches	patches
munches	bunches	pinches	punches

Phonics Pathways: Clear Steps to Easy Reading and Perfect Spelling

When we add "s" to show *ownership* of something, we must first put an *apostrophe* at the end of the word before adding the "s":

Jan has a cat.	It is Jan's cat.
Robin has lunch.	It is Robin's lunch.
Ben has a fish.	It is Ben's fish.

However, to show ownership in words ending with "s," "x," or "z," we only need to add an apostrophe. We *pronounce* the second "s," but do not have to *write* it:

Gus has candy.	It is Gus' candy.
Max has a duck.	It is Max' duck.
Buzz has a wig.	It is Buzz' wig.

The letter "x" sounds exactly like "cks." Read across the page:

tacks	tax	lacks	lax
Bix	box	lox	fox
Max	mix	fax	Rex
ex-it	exit	ex-ist	exist

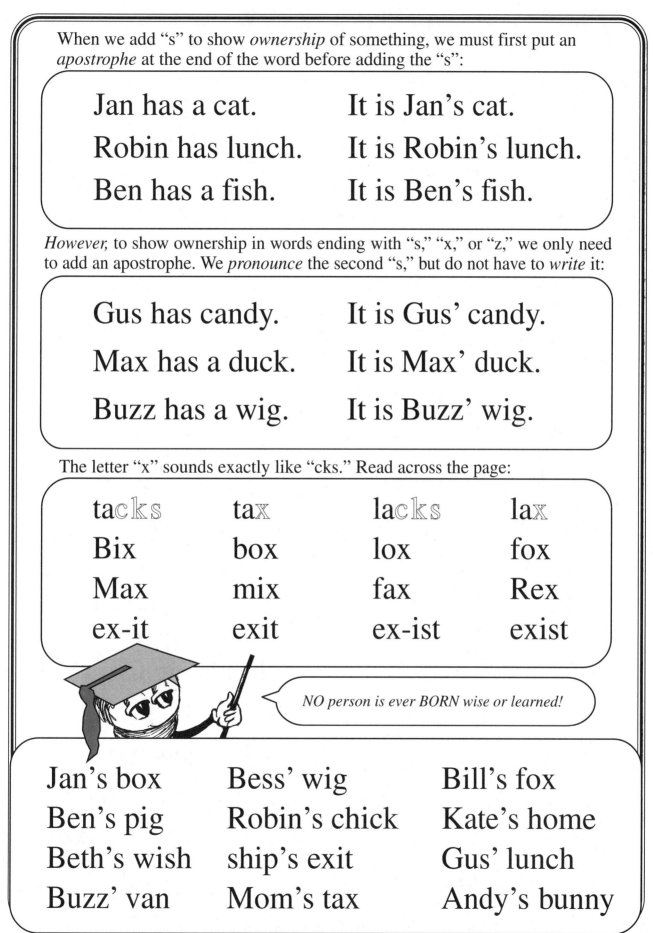

NO person is ever BORN wise or learned!

Jan's box	Bess' wig	Bill's fox
Ben's pig	Robin's chick	Kate's home
Beth's wish	ship's exit	Gus' lunch
Buzz' van	Mom's tax	Andy's bunny

GENERAL REVIEW

Before we try the consonant digraph beginnings on the next page, let's have a general review of what we have learned so far. If you find any endings here that you are UNSURE of, go back to that section and REVIEW them before going on.

Read across the page:

bath	bash	bask	back	batch
math	mash	mask	mack	match

suck	such	muck	much
Rick	rich	rest	bench
king	lunch	ducks	mind
cute	weep	fishes	tasted
sash	sacks	team	liked
sank	math	dishes	biking
handy	misty	Robin	munch
lucky	winner	singing	tidbits
pigpen	catches	fantastic	teaching

Gus' lunch	Robin munches	cute foxes
biking home	peaches hung	Jan's duck
Pete punches	catching robber	Gus moped
colt biting	packing candy	runner puffed
yanking teeth	lacking film	penny sinking
humming tune	Buzz' taxes	baking fish

CONSONANT DIGRAPH BEGINNINGS

Now we shall try putting some of the consonant digraphs we have learned at the *beginning* of a word. The vowel sounds in these lessons will be both short *and* long, so you *may* find yourself working a bit harder to read them! If you find you are working *too hard* over a sound (vowel or ending), go back and review a few words on that page to refresh your memory.

Sh-, sh-

Read across:

sh-am	sham	sh-ut	shut
sh-in	shin	sh-ed	shed
sh-ell	shell	sh-op	shop
sh-un	shun	sh-ank	shank
sh-ock	shock	Sh-elly	Shelly

			SHORT VOWEL
shăll shĭp	shŭn shĕd	shŏp shŭt	
shock shin	shun Shelly	shot shin	
shift shank	shag shall	shift shell	
shut shack	sham shaft	shell sham	

			LONG VOWEL
shāve shēep	shāle shīne	shēet shāde	
shade sheen	Shane shave	sheaf shake	
sheer sheet	shame Shane	shape shone	

*Kindness is the OIL
that takes the FRICTION
out of life!*

hush shop	Hush, let us rush and shop!
shot shin	Dan shot his shin bone.
shame shock	Shelly felt shame and shock.
shall shank	Gus shall munch a sheep shank.
Shane shaky	Shane is in his shaky shed.
shift shine	Golden fish shift and shine.
shall shape	Shall we run and get in shape?
shift shake	Muddy land can shift and shake.
shiny shells	I shall get shiny shells to sell.
shine Shelly's	Sun will shine on Shelly's shack.

No matter WHAT your lot in life may be…
BUILD something on it!
(It's not where you STARTED that counts…
What matters is where you WIND UP!)

Ch-, ch-

Read across:

ch-ip	chip	ch-at	chat
ch-in	chin	ch-um	chum
ch-eck	check	Ch-uck	Chuck
ch-amp	champ	ch-ill	chill

SHORT VOWEL

ch-eek	cheek	ch-oke	choke
ch-ime	chime	ch-ase	chase
ch-ild	child	ch-eer	cheer
ch-eese	cheese	ch-eat	cheat

LONG VOWEL

chămp chĭp   chăt chŭm   chĭll chŏp

chump chug   check chunk   chip chin

Chuck check   chop chink   check chess

chēap pēach   chāse chēese   chōke chēek

chase chime   chide peach   cheat child

cheery child   chimes cheer   chases peach

Speak well of your enemies…
YOU MADE 'EM!

Phonics Pathways: Clear Steps to Easy Reading and Perfect Spelling   121

Chuck chunk	Chuck chops a peach chunk.
chill chugs	Chad got a chill and chugs home.
chip chunk	Chuck's gold chip is a big chunk!
chomps chops	Gus chomps on chips and chops.
check cheery	Check the cheery, chiming bells.
chess cheap	Chuck's chess set is not cheap.
chubby chum	Gus is a chubby, cheery chum.
cheer chum	Cheer up a sad chum, and chat.
Chet chugs	Chet chugs and chases Gus.
chip-munk	A wee chipmunk chits and chats.

*Take your time! Do something each day,
but don't be in a hurry…
Sometimes the most BEAUTIFUL FLOWERS
in the garden are the ones that take
the LONGEST to GROW!*

Here's a *new* digraph blend! We haven't seen this before because it is only used at the *beginning* of words. Read across the page:

Wh-, wh-

wh-en   when   wh-ip   whip

wh-eel   wheel   wh-ale   whale

wh-eat   wheat   wh-ich   which

wh-ile   while   wh-ite   white

whip	whim	when	whiz
which	whisk	wheel	while
wheat	whale	white	whine

There are three words beginning with "wh" that we must learn by sight:

who	whose	what

There are no HOPELESS SITUATIONS…
Only PEOPLE who are hopeless ABOUT them!

whine while	which wheel	white whale
whose whip	who whisks	when whip
when whale	what whiz	while whale
whisk wheat	who whines	what whim

whose white	Whose white wheel is chipped?
which whiz	Which kid is a whiz?
who white	Who chases a white whale?
whose whip	Whose kid has a white whip?
which wheel	Which white wheel is rusty?
whine while	Ann and Dot whine while eating.
which whale	Which whale is big and white?
whose what	Whose cat is whining, and what is its name?
wheat when	Gus munches white wheat when he jogs.
while white	While we had a nap, Gus ate five white cakes.

The WINNER says, "It may be difficult, but it's POSSIBLE!"

The LOSER says, "It may be possible, but it's TOO DIFFICULT!"

The digraph "th" has two sounds.

This is the "soft" sound: **Th-, th-**

th-in   thin   th-ank   thank

th-ump   thump   th-ick   thick

This is the "hard" sound: **T̶h̶=th**

th-is   this   th-at   that

th-em   them   th-ose   those

Here are two sight words beginning with this sound:

> the   they

"T̶H̶-, TH-" REVIEW

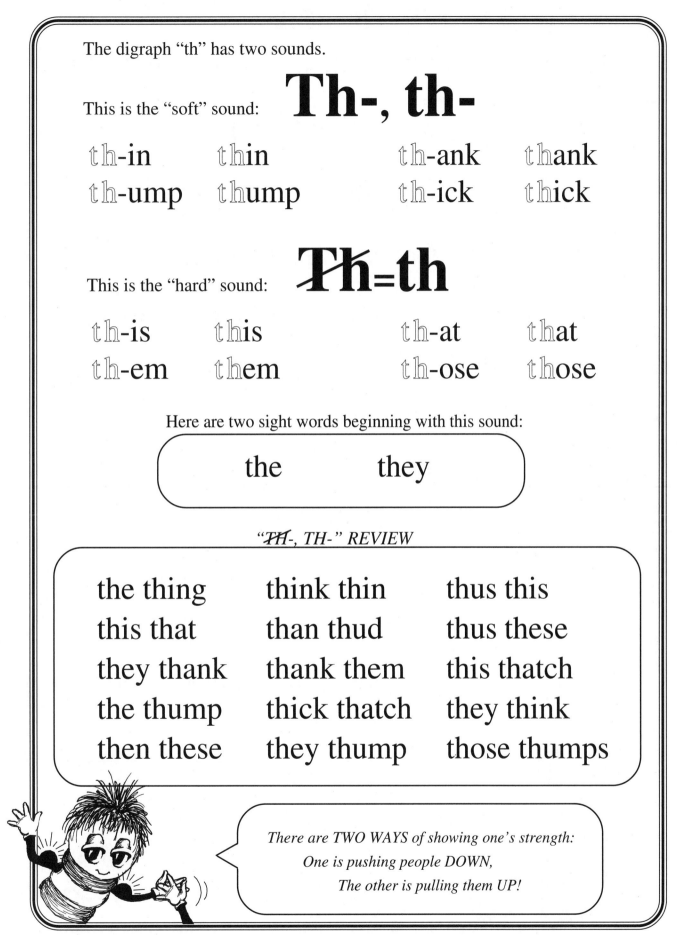

the thing	think thin	thus this
this that	than thud	thus these
they thank	thank them	this thatch
the thump	thick thatch	they think
then these	they thump	those thumps

There are TWO WAYS of showing one's strength:
One is pushing people DOWN,
The other is pulling them UP!

those thin	I think those thin cats need fish.
thing thumps	That thing thumps in the thatch.
thinks thick	Beth thinks this mud is thick.
Cathy the	Cathy takes the thick cake.
thuds thumps	Gus thuds and thumps when he jogs.
then thing	Then the thick thing went thud.
they thank	They thank Cathy for the help with math.
thinks these	Gus thinks he can eat these big, thick, white cakes.
this they	This time they thank those thin kids.

NEVER be afraid to stand up for what YOU think is RIGHT…
People who don't take a stand on SOMETHING Often fall for ANYTHING!

Qu-, qu-

In the English language, "q" is always followed by "u." It sounds like "k" with a "w" added to it:

qu-iz	quiz	qu-ack	quack
qu-it	quit	qu-ick	quick
qu-een	queen	qu-ite	quite
qu-ote	quote	qu-ake	quake

---

quick quake	quit quiz	quote quest
quick quote	queer quilt	queen quit
queen quacks	quest quill	queer quack

---

quickly quake   Run quickly, it is quite a quake!

quacks queerly   The queen duck quacks queerly.

quite quick   Dee makes quite a quick quilt.

quite queer   Gus thinks he feels quite queer.

quotes quite   He quotes quite a quick quiz.

As we grow older, we are a lot like PLANTS...
Some of us go to SEED,
While others keep on GROWING and BLOOMING!

CONSONANT DIGRAPH BEGINNINGS REVIEW

The words in each phrase begin with the *same* consonant digraph:

quick quake	think thin	which wheel
this thing	chit chat	shaky shack
they think	queen quits	Chuck chats
whose whip	cheer chum	ship shines

The words in these phrases begin with *different* consonant digraphs:

that quilt	check shop	quit whine
cheap wheat	they quack	shake Chet
which shop	white quilt	thank who
quick chill	what cheer	wheel chugs

those shaky   Those shaky shacks shift in a quake.

when queen   When shall the thin queen see them?

queer whale   That queer whale chased this ship!

shall grade   Chuck shall grade Chad's chess quiz.

whose chat   Whose chums chat while shopping?

quit chubby   Gus thinks he will quit chasing those quick, chubby, white sheep.

> *We can't go back and change our BEGINNING,*
> *but we can begin to change our ENDING…*
> *Everybody has a FUTURE as well as a PAST!*

Now we shall learn double-consonant *beginnings*. You will not need to read all of the vowels and blends first, unless double-consonant beginnings prove difficult Then read *all* of the blends—*DO YOUR EYEROBICS!* Read across:

bl-

a	la	bla	black
e	le	ble	bled
i	li	bli	bliss
o	lo	blo	block
u	lu	blu	blush

Always THINK for YOURSELF... or SOMEONE ELSE will do it FOR you!

less bless	led bled	lush blush
lend blend	lock block	lack black

fl-

a	la	fla	flag
e	le	fle	fled
i	li	fli	flip
o	lo	flo	flop
u	lu	flu	flung

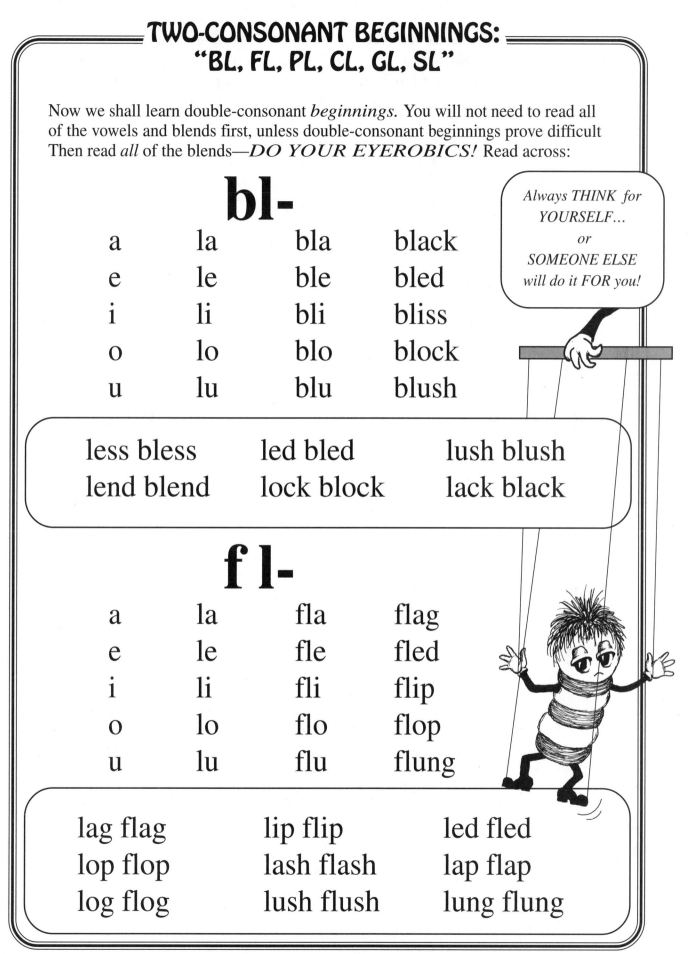

lag flag	lip flip	led fled
lop flop	lash flash	lap flap
log flog	lush flush	lung flung

Practicing your eyerobics will make your eyes *so* much stronger, and better able to move *smoothly* and *easily* across the page, just as aerobics will make your *body* muscles a lot stronger, so that you can *run* faster!

pl-

a	la	pla	plan
e	le	ple	plenty
i	li	pli	plink
o	lo	plo	plot
u	lu	plu	plush

SOME MINDS are like CONCRETE... ALL MIXED UP

lug plug	lot plot	lush plush
lank plank	luck pluck	lent plenty
link plink	lane plane	lump plump

cl-

a	la	cla	clap
e	le	cle	clef
i	li	cli	cliff
o	lo	clo	clock
u	lu	clu	club

and PERMANENTLY SET!

lass class	lip clip	lap clap
lamp clamp	lock clock	lick click
luck cluck	lank clank	lump clump

gl-

a	la	gla	glad
e	le	gle	glen
i	li	gli	glint
o	lo	glo	glob
u	lu	glu	glum

We CAN'T

lad glad	Len glen	lint glint
lop glop	land gland	lob glob
lass glass	laze glaze	lean glean

turn BACK the clock... but we CAN wind it UP again!

sl-

a	la	sla	slam
e	le	sle	sled
i	li	sli	slid
o	lo	slo	slot
u	lu	slu	slug

lot slot	lip slip	lid slid
link slink	led sled	lap slap
lash slash	lug slug	lick slick
lime slime	lump slump	lush slush

The beginning double-consonants in each phrase are *different*. Read across:

blot clot	plush slush	clap flap
flip clip	flop plop	flip slip
fling sling	flint glint	bled fled
blush flush	blink slink	clan plan
plunk clunk	glass class	slap flap
block clock	black slacks	flash slash

The long-vowel sounds in each phrase are the same. Read across:

blame flame	glide slide	plead sleep
gleam clean	bleak sleet	glaze plate
pleat sleeve	glade blaze	sleek fleet

The beginning double-consonants in each phrase are the *same*. Read across:

blink blush	flash flag	slip slush
flip flop	plan plot	flung fleck
clip club	sled slide	clasp clock
glass glob	clung cliff	black blaze
plush plum	plump pleat	Blake bluff
slump sleep	fled flame	glum Glen
plenty plants	plush plane	slimy slug

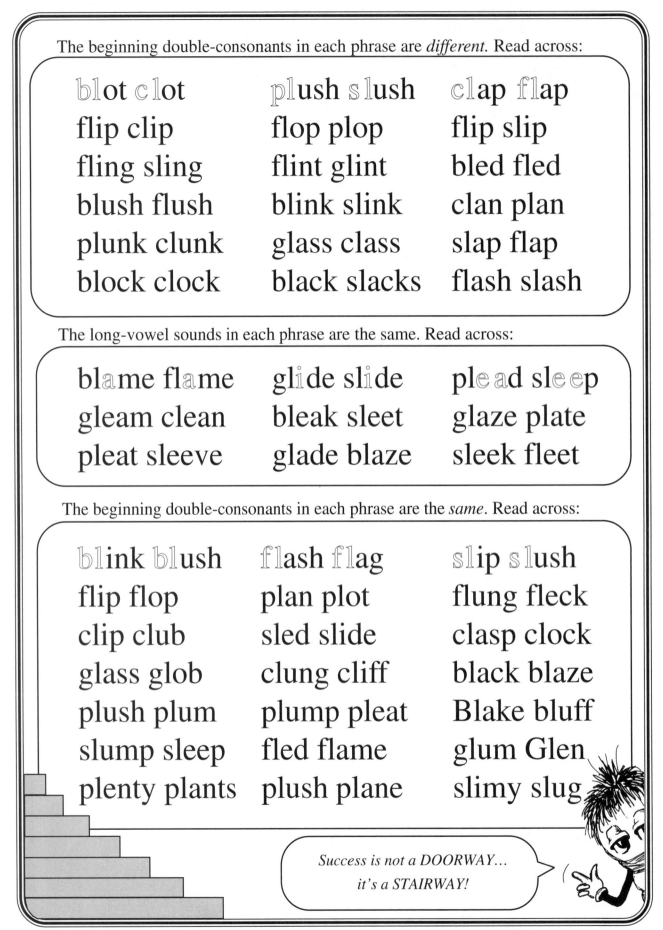

Success is not a DOORWAY…
it's a STAIRWAY!

flips flings	She flips and flings glass blocks.
slipped black	We slipped on black, slick slush.
please blot	Please blot that black ink fleck.
sled slips	His sled slips as it glides in sleet.
glad flunk	He is glad not to flunk this class.
fled flashy	Glen fled with his flashy clock.
clink clank	"Clink, clank, clunk," slid the car.
gladly plucks	Glen gladly plucks plump plums.
slip slide	I slip and I slide in the slick glen.
slugs plop	Big black slugs plop on his plants.
sleepy slumps	Sleepy Gus plops and slumps into his plush, black bed.

Sometimes a good educational channel is found by clicking "OFF"!

Now let's have some *fun!* You've been working hard and deserve a break. First, read these words. They *seem* to be very different but have one thing in common—they are all *palindromes.* Can you guess what that is? (Turn upside down.)

pup	eve	dad
did	sees	noon
deed	peep	toot
level	refer	madam

A palindrome is a word that reads the same *backward or forward!*

What is the very *longest* one-syllable word in the English language?
(Answer upside down.)   Actually there are TWO: "strengths" and "screeched."

What is the shortest word that contains *all* the vowels—a, e, i, o, u?
(Answer upside down.)   Sequoia!

And now, here is a sentence made *only* from single letters and numbers. Can you decode this "secret sentence"?   (The answer is upside down.)

KT, I C U R YY 4 LC.   "Katie, I see you are too wise for Elsie."

Last, read the sentence below. Hold it upside down and look at its reflection in a mirror. Read it again. *Surprise!*

BECKIE KIDDED DIXIE

It takes 72 muscles to FROWN and only 14 to SMILE...
... and besides, smiling adds to your "FACE" VALUE!
(If you see someone without a smile, give him one of YOURS!)

sm-

a	ma	sma	smash
e	me	sme	smell
i	mi	smi	Smith
o	mo	smo	smock
u	mu	smu	smug

mile smile	mock smock	mug smug
mash smash	Mack smack	mite smite

sn-

a	na	sna	snap
e	ne	sne	snell
i	ni	sni	snip
o	no	sno	snob
u	nu	snu	snuff

nap snap	nub snub	nip snip
nag snag	Nell snell	nob snob

SPECIAL NOTE to students still reversing letters, or finding it hard to read: Please begin every lesson from now on by going back to one of the pages in this section and reading across one group of words, from the short vowel to the whole word It will be a GREAT eyerobic warm up!

st-

a	ta	sta	stack
e	te	ste	stem
i	ti	sti	stick
o	to	sto	stop
u	tu	stu	stuck

tab stab	tiff stiff	top stop
tack stack	tan Stan	take stake
tuck stuck	tick stick	tock stock

sp-

a	pa	spa	span
e	pe	spe	spell
i	pi	spi	spill
o	po	spo	spot
u	pu	spu	spun

pat spat	pit spit	pot spot
pill spill	pan span	pine spine
pun spun	poke spoke	peak speak

sc-, sk-

Do you remember when we learned (on page 51) that the "k" sound is spelled with a "k" when it comes before "e" or "i," and with a "c" when it comes before an "a," "o," or "u"?

The same thing usually happens when you put an "s" before the "k":

a	ca	sca	scat
e	ke	ske	sketch
i	ki	ski	skip
o	co	sco	Scotch
u	cu	scu	scum

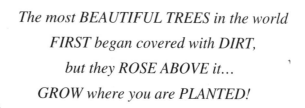

The most BEAUTIFUL TREES in the world
FIRST began covered with DIRT,
but they ROSE ABOVE it...
GROW where you are PLANTED!

cat scat	kin skin	kit skit
kid skid	Kip skip	cab scab
can scan	Kate skate	kill skill
cope scope	cone scone	cuff scuff

smug Smith	smell smoke	smash smock	**sm**
smoky smell	smear smock	Smith smile	
sneaky snake	snake sneeze	snip snag	**sn**
sniff snack	snatch sneak	snob snubs	
stiff stems	stick stuck	stand still	**st**
stove steams	stone stack	steel stake	
spill spot	speed spin	spank spine	**sp**
spade spike	speak spell	spoke spend	
scab skin	skunk skids	scuff scalp	**sc,**
scale scope	skate skids	skip skim	**sk**

> *I do reveal the WAY that I FEEL*
> *By the things that I SAY and DO…*
> *By CHANGING the things that I SAY and DO*
> *I can CHANGE the way that I FEEL!*

stiff spine	smell stale	skate skids
snatch snack	skid stone	snake slides
sneaky snob	skip stack	smug smile
sneeze smoke	stove spills	Scott sniffs
Smith speaks	stand speech	smelly skunk

sneeze smell   I sneeze when I smell smoke.

smug fleas   Smug fleas sneak and stab Skip.

sneaky snakes   Sneaky snakes skid and stop.

stiff snobs   The stiff snobs sniff and snuff.

spilled stink   Spilled eggs stink and smell.

Spot snoops   Spot snoops, sniffs, and snuffs.

snatch stack   Snatch that stack of stiff sticks.

sticky spill   The sticky spill left a black spot.

step spin   We step, spin, skip, and skid!

stop smug   Stop that smug sneak. Scat!

spunky stands   Spunky Spot stands still.

stacks sticky   Gus smells stacks and stacks of sticky scones. Snack time!

In LIFE, as in RESTAURANTS, we must sometimes swallow things we DON'T LIKE... Just because it COMES ON THE PLATE!

Read down each column:

br	cr	dr	fr	gr	pr	tr
ra	ra	ra	ra	ra	ra	ra
bra	cra	dra	fra	gra	pra	tra
brat	crab	drag	Fran	Grant	pram	tram
re	re	re	re	re	re	re
bre	cre	dre	fre	gre	pre	tre
Brett	crest	dress	fresh	Greg	press	trend
ri	ri	ri	ri	ri	ri	ri
bri	cri	dri	fri	gri	pri	tri
brick	crib	drip	frisk	grip	print	trim
ro	ro	ro	ro	ro	ro	ro
bro	cro	dro	fro	gro	pro	tro
Bron	crop	drop	frock	groggy	prop	trot
ru	ru	ru	ru	ru	ru	ru
bru	cru	dru	fru	gru	pru	tru
brush	crush	drum	frump	grump	prūne	truck

FORGIVENESS is like MAGIC…
It COOLS the hurt but it WARMS the heart!

The words in each phrase have the *same* vowel sound. Read across:

drag pram	Fred frets	drop crock
grip slip	crank prank	crush truck
brush crust	grab crab	cram tram
press dress	drop slop	Fran tracks
trick stick	free cream	frame grate
trade crate	green creek	bride pride

The words in these phrases have *different* vowel sounds. Read across:

pram slips	frisky Grant	Fred trips
crabby Greg	Trixie drags	trim brush
Fran drops	crank crib	trick Frank
Trudy grabs	cranky Brad	grassy crest
fresh crock	crunch brick	prop truck
cliff cracks	drop crutch	grim brink
trade drinks	crave brunch	brave Grant
green grape	dream bride	free prune
crate broke	prime grade	creek froze

*I hope you're remembering to review the words in each lesson until you are able to read and write them easily. If you make a mistake, try again and just keep going… Remember… **NOBODY'S PERFECT**. (That's why PENCILS have ERASERS!)*

The words in each phrase have the *same* short vowel and ending. Read across:

truck stuck	grab crab	fling sling
flop plop	trip grip	black slacks
cramp clamp	flap trap	press dress
track cracks	slick trick	stock clock
smug slug	fled sled	slink plink
smash flash	snip drip	flick brick

The words in these phrases have *different* short vowels and endings:

sled spins	crush bricks	smack slug
scuff slacks	pluck crop	grumpy Fred
Grant frets	skip class	black truck

The words in each phrase have the *same* long vowel and ending:

grope slope	grime slime	steer clear
steam cream	Clive drive	troll stole
blame frame	clone stone	dream cream
drapes grapes	blaze glaze	bride glide

The words in these phrases have *different* vowels and endings:

smug bride	glass clean	fresh cream
crunch stone	speed skate	Grant sleepy
trust Jane	brush frame	blame trick

Beware the TONGUE...it's very WET and likely to SLIP!

Here are *two* pages of review! Notice that the sentences on the next page are longer. Take it easy—you don't have to read them quickly. These sentences are more complicated, so don't get discouraged if you do slow down a bit when reading them. Everyone does. However, if you are having *too* difficult a time reading them, go back to reading them as suggested on page 74. It is important that you always feel *challenged*—but never *frustrated!*

(Remember to check out the games and activities beginning on page 250— They're a great way to reinforce learning and make it fun at the same time!)

crabby Greg	Crabby Greg drags and frets.
Brent drinks	Brent drinks milk in the grass.
trucks crunch	Trucks drop and crunch bricks.
fresh frock	A fresh frock is a dream dress.
Frank grumpy	Frank is grumpy and groggy.
Grant crave	Grant and Fred crave brunch.
Fran crutches	Fran drops the broken crutches.
Trixie frisky	Trixie is frisky and trots, but trips.

The BEST VITAMIN for MAKING FRIENDS is "B–1."

snake glides	The sneaky snake slides and glides on the slick path
trip grab	I trip and grab the brink of the grim cliff.
sticky slinky	Smash this sticky, slinky, green slug. It clings!
grabs Grant's	Fred grabs Grant's frisky, tricky, black ducks.
crabby groggy	Fran is crabby and groggy, and slumps into bed.
flung branch	Greg flung the branch in a clump of green grass.
glide swift	We glide, slip, and slide with these swift skates.
sniffs brunch	Gus sniffs brunch and drops his glass of fresh milk.
grumpy cranky	Brent and Trudy trick grumpy, cranky Brad. He frets.

WHEW. . . Glad THAT's done!

So far we have learned about the two sounds vowels usually make: the short sound, as in "rat," and the long sound, as in "rate."

When a vowel is followed by the letter "r" it makes *another* sound, which is neither short nor long. This sound has been modified, or changed, by the "r."

är=ar

This is the diacritical mark for an "r" modified "a" sound. It is called an "umlaut." Read down:

ark	art	card	are
bark	cart	hard	arm
dark	part	yard	harm
lark	tart	lard	charm
mark	dart	chard	yarn
park	mart	carp	barn
spark	start	harp	parch
shark	chart	tarp	farm
Clark	smart	sharp	farm-yard

yarn art	arms are	part lard
hard part	dark park	barn farm
smart carp	start harp	mark tarp
card shark	Mark bark	chard tart
lark charm	chart dart	cart spark
Clark's ark	shark harm	sharp yard

FORGIVE and FORGET! SOUR GRAPES make BAD WINE.

Phonics Pathways: Clear Steps to Easy Reading and Perfect Spelling

ôr=or

This is the diacritical mark for an "r" modified "o" sound. It is called a "circumflex." There are *six different spellings* of this sound! Read down:

or	cord	sort	worn
for	corn	sport	torn
fork	scorn	short	horn
pork	porch	snort	born
cork	torch	form	morn
stork	north	storm	doc-tor

ôr=ar

("Ar" always sounds like "ôr" when it follows a "w.")

war	ward	wart	warm
award	warn	warp	warm-up

Take a lesson from the MOSQUITO…
It never sits around WAITING
for an opening…
IT MAKES ONE!

worn horn	fork pork	torn cork
short stork	warm sport	war story
sort award	short war	born morn
storm north	snort forth	warn dorm
warp form	scorn glory	wart doctor
short warmup	torch scorch	warm porch

ôr=oor

| floor | floor-ing | door | in-door |

ôr=ore

| core | tore | store | score |
| more | lore | shore | bore |

ôr=our

| four | pour | course | fourth |

ôr=oar

| oar | board | roar | soar |

> Here is a sentence using ALL SIX spelling patterns for this sound:
>
> ## Four more warm storks soar indoors.
>
> *Copy this sentence over on paper, and circle each spelling pattern. Check to be sure you found them all. (It might also be fun to try writing your OWN sentence, choosing your words from each spelling pattern!)*

door horn	court Dor	for store
pour more	north lore	short oar
four doors	worn floor	corn core
soar shore	roar snort	store door
floor board	tore board	dorm floor
coarse pork	wore more	fourth torch
warm storm	porch floor	short course

"ÄR" AND "ÔR" REVIEW

four warm	Gus eats chard, carp, pork, corn, and warm shark for lunch.
more chores	Robin has four more hard chores she must start.
horns awards	The four horns are for Mark, and more awards are for Clark.
doctor snores	The old doctor sits on his warm porch and snores and snores.
doors warped	The four doors in the dark barn are warped and torn.
course start	Of course she can take four more courses and start sports.
horse snorts	His horse snorts and roars at the short stork in the yard.
warn sharks	Warn Clark that four smart sharks tore his floor board.

To really appreciate the dignity and beauty
of an OLD FACE
you have to READ BETWEEN THE LINES!

There can be *five spelling patterns* for the "er" sound! The diacritical mark for this sound is "ŭr." If you look up "her" in the dictionary, for example, it will show the pronunciation as "hŭr." Read down each spelling pattern:

ŭr=er	ŭr=ir	ŭr=ur
her	sir	urn
herd	stir	turn
pert	fir	burn
Bert	bird	hurt
jerk	birth	fur
term	mirth	cur
berth	girl	curl
Herb	dirt	curb
clerk	firm	purr
fern	first	lurk
perch	thirst-y	murk-y

It's what you learn AFTER you KNOW IT ALL that COUNTS!

curb dirt	her turn	burn fir
fur herd	hurt fern	jerk urn
Sir Herb	turn berth	pert cur
first birth	murky fir	Bert lurk
Bert purr	bird perch	firm curl
thirsty girl	firm mirth	girl clerk

Here are two more spelling patterns for this sound. "Or" says "ur" whenever it has a "w" in front of it. Read across the page:

ur=or

work	word	worm
worst	worth	wor-ship
world	worse	wors-en
worm-y	worth-y	wor-sted

ur=ear

earn	learn	yearn
heard	search	earth

Now here is a sentence using ALL FIVE "ur" spelling patterns:

Bert's earth-worms stir and turn.

Copy this sentence, and circle each of the five "ur" spelling patterns. Now try writing a different sentence, choosing your own words from as many of these groups as you can think of.

"ER, IR, UR, OR, EAR=UR" REVIEW

her work	Herb hurt	earn fur
girl turn	her word	Gert purr
early bird	dirty worm	first work
earth first	learn work	girl heard
worst burn	worthy urn	jerk perch
search world	thirsty fern	worm curl
worthy search	per-fect pearl	burn worsen

Here is a review of all the "ur" spelling patterns. They can be tricky to learn, and it's good to take time to know them. Read down each spelling group:

er   ir   ur   or   ear

er	ir	ur	or	ear
her	sir	urn	work	earn
herd	stir	turn	worth	learn
pert	fir	burn	worm	earth
Bert	bird	hurt	world	heard
jerk	birth	fur	word	pearl
term	mirth	cur	worst	ear-ly
fern	girl	curl	worth	search
Herb	dirt	curb	wor-ry	searched
clerk	firm	purr	worth-y	search-er
per-fect	first	lurk	work-er	learn-er

her turn	firm dirt	girl learn
world search	earn pearl	pert Herb
hurt cur	perfect fern	Bert purr
first birth	early bird	worthy fir
worst herd	firm earth	Herb clerk
earthworm	girl worry	heard bird
jerk urn	curb dirt	worm curl
clerk learn	worker heard	searcher burn

Sometimes people are lonely because they build WALLS instead of BRIDGES…

Let's try reading some multisyllable words again, just as we did on page 113. We'll also incorporate some of the "r"-modified vowels we have just learned. It's fun to "build" words from "blocks" of syllables! Read down each group:

hard	sharp	art
hard-en	sharp-en	ar-tist
hard´-en-er	sharp´-en-er	ar-tis´-tic
car	form	su
car-pen	per-form	su-per
car´-pen-ter	per-form´-er	su´-per-man
or	croc	al
or-na	croc-o	al-li
or´-na-ment	croc´-o-dile	al´li-ga-tor

hardener	sharpener	artistic
carpenter	performer	superman
ornament	crocodile	alligator

See you later, alligator…
After a while, crocodile!

If you find it difficult to read the longer words, try covering up most of the word first, and then SLOWLY move the paper over while you read each syllable. Some people find this helpful. What do YOU think?... And, by the way,

Don't just WAIT for your ship to come in... SWIM OUT TO IT!

search stirs

We search for our pert kitty,
   Pearl. She stirs and purrs.

heard perfect

I heard that her work is perfect.
   She learns and earns a lot.

yearns world

The girl yearns and searches
   for peace in her world.

earth-worms

Bert heard that Herb will search
   early for his earthworms.

thirsty berth

Thirsty Gert curls and turns
   in her firm berth.

first learns

First, Gus learns to stir and
   turn his beef. It burns!

Fern's dirty

We must first clean Fern's
   dirty but pert bird.

FEAR less, HOPE more…
EAT less, CHEW more…
WHINE less, BREATHE more…
TALK less, SAY more…
HATE less, LOVE more…
AND ALL GOOD THINGS ARE YOURS!

The words in each phrase have the *same* "r" modified vowel sound:

Mark park	Bert purr	born morn
girl earn	hard part	larks are
worst dirt	more corn	farm yard
learn work	start harp	horn worn
award store	firm perch	four forks
worm curl	chart shark	thirsty fern

The words in each phrase have *different* "r" modified vowel sounds:

Bert roar	arm hurt	sort pearls
torch burn	pork tart	Gert charm
smart bird	girl born	store pearls
worst dorm	shark curl	more chard
Clark learn	north star	warm perch
search park	dark porch	murky morn

learned four   Pearl learned that four ferns in the yard got torn in the storm.

part morning   Part of the burn on Herb's arm turned worse in the morning.

You have TWO EARS and only ONE MOUTH...
LISTEN TWICE as much as TALK!

This section of the book will introduce some other ways to spell long-vowel sounds. We shall be learning the *long-vowel digraphs.*

A digraph, as you remember, is two letters that make one sound. We have studied consonant digraphs such as "sh" and "th," and we have also learned two long-vowel digraphs: "ee" and "ea." Now we shall learn the *rest* of them!

It may take a while to learn how to read and spell these digraphs, so remember to take *all the time you need* with each one. Also remember that when there are so many different ways to spell a sound, at first it might be best to dictate these words by *family*, as presented on page 66. They will be easier to read and spell this way.

Eventually you must be able to read and write these words randomly, in any sentence Being able to *read* these words is the most important thing for now—you can come back to this book for more detailed spelling lessons later. When you *are* ready to teach spelling, however, do check out *Spelling Strategies* on page 238. It's an easy step-by-step guide on exactly how to teach spelling with *Phonics Pathways.*

As in the last section, the review sentences are longer and use more multisyllable words. It is quite *natural* if you temporarily slow down a little bit when you read them. You are stretching and expanding your reading skills!

There *is one thing* you should watch for. If you find yourself really stumbling over the *same kind* of sounds, then you need to go back to that section of the book and take time out to review it. It is common for this to happen, and is the *true test* of whether or not you know these rules well enough for them to be automatic when reading them. It does not matter if you are just *slowed down*— speed comes with practice—but you should not have to *struggle* with each individual word. It's very important to work at a *challenging* but *comfortable* pace!

T E A C H I N G   T I P S: Those who are still struggling with eye-tracking might prefer to continue reading these sentences using the method shown on page 74. And *please* remember to do your eyerobic warm-ups if it *is* difficult for you! (You didn't forget what they *are,* did you? See page 136!)

Remember to incorporate the activities and games in the appendix (from page 250). They will really reinforce learning and make it *so* much more *enjoyable* at the same time!

Why not start a NEW DIET?
No more EATING your own words,
SWALLOWING your pride,
or putting your FOOT in your mouth!

ā=ai

We use the long "a" diacritical mark for the "ai, ay" digraphs, since they have this sound. Read down:

aid	rain	ail	wait
maid	main	bail	bait
paid	gain	jail	trait
raid	vain	sail	faint
laid	pain	nail	saint
braid	Spain	pail	paint
aim	brain	Gail	taint
maim	drain	fail	stain
claim	train	frail	chain
plain	strain	trail	com-plaint

wait jail	laid rail	aid raid
paid maid	maim nail	pain strain
aim bait	stain rain	vain Gail
Gail braid	plain chain	sail Spain
saint faint	brain drain	frail trail
paint pail	main train	claim gain

Keep your FACE to the SUNSHINE, and you will NEVER SEE the SHADOWS!

ā=ay

(It is spelled like this when it appears at the *end* of a word. Read down:)

Jay	lay	way	ray
may	play	sway	pray
say	clay	a-way	gray
stay	slay	way-side	tray
tray	flay	mid-way	fray
stray	de-lay	day	bray
to-day	lay-er	day-time	hay
cray-fish	lay-a-way	holi-day	hay-stack

Test your STRENGTH by lifting a HEAVY WEIGHT off someone's shoulders!

gray day	Kay may	play clay
pay today	Ray betray	tray sway
spray hay	stray crayfish	May holiday

"AI, AY=Ā" REVIEW

pray rain	mail train	hay grain
play clay	pay maid	frail Kay
slay tail	pail sway	say Spain
main trail	spray paint	gray day
aid crayfish	wait haystack	stay holiday

Gail frail

Gail is frail and must not play on a rainy day.

mail train

The mail train is running late. Shall we wait at the gate?

tray crayfish

Gus laid his tray with crayfish on the main table today.

pay plain

Say, who can I pay for this plain gray cake tray?

Kay lays

Kay lays chains and nails in the pail on the clay trail.

paint gray

Please paint this ship plain gray. We will wait and sail later.

Gail stay

Gail can stay late. May we play with clay while waiting?

trail freeway

Wait! I see the main trail faintly near the freeway.

LAUGHTER is a tranquilizer with **NO SIDE EFFECTS!**

Sometimes the "ie" digraph sounds like long "e." (We have already had the "ee" and "ea" digraphs.) but are included here this sound.

"I" and "y" are not digraphs because they both have Read down the page:

ē=ie

thief	pier	field
chief	tier	yield
grief	grieve	shield
brief	re-lieve	Ka-tie
fiend	be-lieve	Las-sie
fierce	re-trieve	Con-nie
pierce	a-chieve	Deb-bie

ē=i   marine   machine

-y=-ies

We have already had "y" endings on page 68. When we make a word with "y" ending plural (more than one), we must first change the "y" to "i," and then add "-es." Read across the page:

pan-sy	pan-sies	du-ty	du-ties
ru-by	ru-bies	pen-ny	pen-nies
par-ty	par-ties	ba-by	ba-bies
car-ry	car-ries	hur-ry	hur-ries
pup-py	pup-pies	kit-ty	kit-ties

thief quickly	grieve kitty
chief armies	relieve Katie
shield puppy	achieve duty
carry pansies	fiend hurries
believe priest	Debbie slowly
Connie parties	Lassie's babies
Marine achieves	pennies machine

Katie briefly	Katie and Debbie run briefly in the field of pansies.
puppies shield	Ten puppies hurry and shield baby Jackie.
believe marine	I believe the chief Marine will be funny and brief.
carries tiers	Gus carries a party cake with cherries and ten tiers.
hand-ker-chief	Katie forgot her handkerchief. She quickly retrieves it.

The person who makes NO MISTAKES usually does not make ANYTHING!

Here "ie," "ui," and "uy" have a *long "i"* sound. "Y" is not a digraph but is included because here it has the long "i" sound. Read across the page:

ī=ie, y

try	tries	dry	dries	fry	fries
fly	flies	cry	cries	sky	skies

lie	pie	tie	die
my	by	spy	shy
why	rye	eye	Clyde
type	typ-ist	style	styl-ish
ty-coon	ty-rant	ply	ply-wood
dy-nam-ic		dy-na-mite	

ī=uy

guy	buy
	buyer

ī=ui

guile	beguile
guise	guide	disguise

To handle YOURSELf, use your HEAD…to handle OTHERS, use your HEART!

try pie	shy guy	rye pies
tie die	my eye	fly skies
spy tries	buyer lies	guide Clyde
by typist	my typing	spies crying
disguise eyes	stylish guy	buy plywood

why Clyde   Why did Clyde cry? He tried lying.

tried eyes   She tried flying the kite by my eyes.

guide flies   Guide my fine jet as it flies with
                             style in the wild sky.

cried pies   Gus cried and cried while his fried
                             rye pies dried.

try disguise   Why did Clyde try buying my spy
                             disguise?

sly guy   The sly guy tried spying by my vine.

typist buys   My shy typist buys stylish ties.

die crying   Why did Clyde's fine, shy kitten
                             die? He is crying.

tycoon fries   The shy tycoon cried as he spilled
                             french fries on his tie-dyed pants.

TWO PEOPLE looked at a rose bush:
One was ANGRY because the ROSES had THORNS,
the other was HAPPY because the THORNS had ROSES!

These sounds are all long "o." Read down each column:

$\bar{o}$=oa	$\bar{o}$=oe	$\bar{o}$=ow
oat	toe	tow
boat	hoe	bow
goat	foe	bowl
load	Joe	low
loaf	goes	slow
road	hoes	flow
roast	Joe's	grow

hol-low   yel-low   pil-low   win-dow

fol-low   fel-low   wil-low   shad-ow

toast loaf	row boat
Joe's goat	roast oats
crow goes	coast road
soap floats	load bowl
toad croaks	yellow hoe
low shadow	fellow goes
hollow float	foam pillow
Joan follows	bowl slowly
willow blows	show window

FAITH is what helps us live between the TRAPEZES!

boasts shows	Joan boasts and shows her load of yellow bows.
loaf float	We like to loaf, float, and lie low in Joe's hollow boat.
flows slowly	This low river flows slowly until it goes by the coast road.
willow blow	These willow trees blow in the snow and grow slowly.
follows grown	Joan follows Joe's grown goat. It goes most slowly.
show toad	Show Moe the old toad croaking on my yellow pillow!
roast loaf	Gus likes roast meat loaf, toast, and oats in a bowl for lunch.

Sometimes we change not because we see the LIGHT but because we feel the HEAT!

Here are a variety of spelling patterns for long "u" words. Read down each column:

ōo=oo

too (Means "also" or "extremely.")
soon
spoon
spool
goof
stoop
moose
moon
fool
food
choose
drool
smooth
stool
zoom
tooth
proof

ōo=ew

new
dew
grew
drew
stew
strew
Lew
flew
blew
news
chew

yōo=ew

few
mew
hew
skew

ōo=ue

true
glue
blue
flue
Sue
due

ōo=ui

Sometimes the long "u" sound is spelled "ui":

fruit
fruit-cake
juice
bruise
cruise
suit
suit-able
suit-case

ōo=ou

Here are a few long "u" words which are spelled "ou." Read across the page:

| you | youth | your | un-couth |
| soup | pouf | group | mousse |

ōo = o

And finally, sometimes "o" can sound like long "u":

do   to *(Means "action" or "direction.")*   two* *(Means "number." "W" is silent.)*

prove   im-prove   whom

move   movie   move-ment

*Note special spelling of the number "two."

Here is a sentence using *all* of the spelling patterns for "ōo":

Your two blue moose stoop to chew fruit.

Copy this sentence and circle each one of these spelling patterns. Now write your own sentence, using as many "oo" spelling patterns as you can think of.

The words in each phrase have the same long "u" spelling. Read across:

soon moon	Sue due	youth group
blue glue	to prove	fool drool
Lew grew	news flew	fruit juice
loose tooth	goof proof	your soup
chew stew	cruise suits	do im-prove
tooth drool	Lew flew	do move-ment
moose stoop	zoom moon	bruise suit-case
improve movie	choose spoon	suit-able cruise

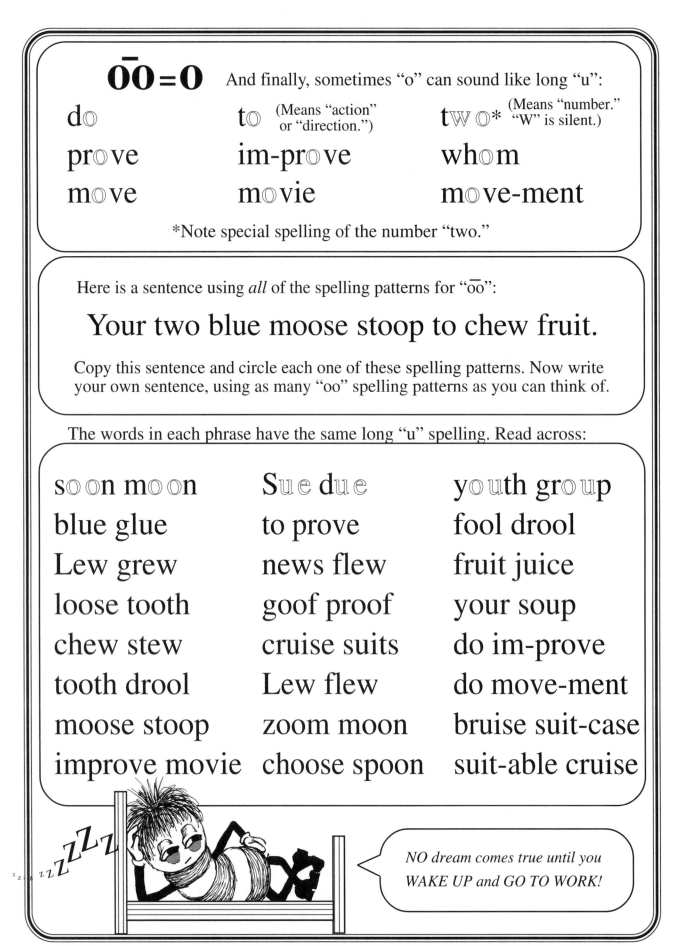

NO dream comes true until you WAKE UP and GO TO WORK!

two suits	fool Lew	too few
goof proof	new suit	to cruise
two moose	to movie	Lew drew
chew fruit	do choose	new tooth
bruise fruit	crew flew	blue moon
choose suit	soon stew	brew juice
few moose	Luke drew	blue spoon
youth group	Sue prove	drool soup
smooth food	move stool	bruise two

two moose Two big moose soon grew
       blue under the new moon.

Sue drools Baby Sue drools soup and soon
      has goo on her new suit!

snoop blue A goose stooped to snoop by
      the blue pool and then flew.

smooth fruit The smooth fruit juice is too
      cool on Lew's loose tooth.

chooses cruise Gus chooses a cruise with food
      to chew and a movie, too.

Sometimes we HAVE to take a big step…
We can't cross a chasm in TWO SMALL JUMPS!

LONG-VOWEL DIGRAPH REVIEW

The long-vowel digraphs in each group of words have the same sound. Read across:

wait train	play clay	rain today	**a**
spray grain	paint tray	gray trail	
frail Kay	plain pail	bait snail	
shield penny	carry babies	marine yield	**e**
believe Lassie	Debbie's grief	kitty hurries	
Connie carries	shield puppies	Katie's party	
buy pies	tried typing	guide Clyde	**i**
spies lied	rye dries	tried fries	
why cry	my plywood	flying skies	
follow goat	tow boat	hold toe	**o**
yellow pillow	willow grow	soak road	
Joe's shadow	flow slowly	load boat	
blue moon	chew fruit	move soup	**u**
smooth juice	moose soup	Sue prove	
youth snoop	group cruise	grew tooth	

These words contain a *variety* of long-vowel digraphs. Read across the page:

fool spies	juice stain	Joe flew
Lassie tried	chief typist	buy pail
babies grow	choose paint	rain today
marine guide	frail puppies	blue moose
pansies blow	disguise Debbie	show movie

On page 51 we learned that the "k" sound is spelled with a "c" when it is followed by "a," "o," or "u," and with a "k" when it is followed by "e" or "i."

What happens if we *do* put "c" before "e" or "i"? It has an "s" sound!

s=ce

cent	cell	cel-e-brate
cer-ti-fy	cen-ter	cel-ery
cease	celebrate	ce-ment

Whenever a word ends with "ce," the "e" is silent. Read down:

ace	prince	ice	twice
pace	prance	rice	spice
lace	Grace	lice	price
face	trace	nice	slice
mace	brace	mice	mince
face	space	dance	since
fleece	place	dunce	choice

You may find the WORST ENEMY or BEST FRIEND within YOURSELF!

mince ice	nice face	since race
place cent	spice rice	center lace
pace twice	trace Grace	price celery
cement cell	certify dunce	Grace dance
cease dance	prince prance	ace celebrate

"Ci" usually has a short "i" sound, but it *can* have a long "i" sound as well:

s=ci, cy

civ-il	cin-der	cin-e-ma	ci-der (long "i")
cir-cus	cir-cle	cit-y	cinema

"Cy" is usually pronounced with a long "i":

cy-cle   cy-clone   cy-press

civil cinema   cycle cinema   cypress city
cyclone circle   cinder cider   circle circus

This brings us to *another* long-vowel digraph. When the "ie" long "e" digraph has a "c" in front of it, the spelling usually changes. It becomes "ei." Knowing this rule will *really help* your spelling!

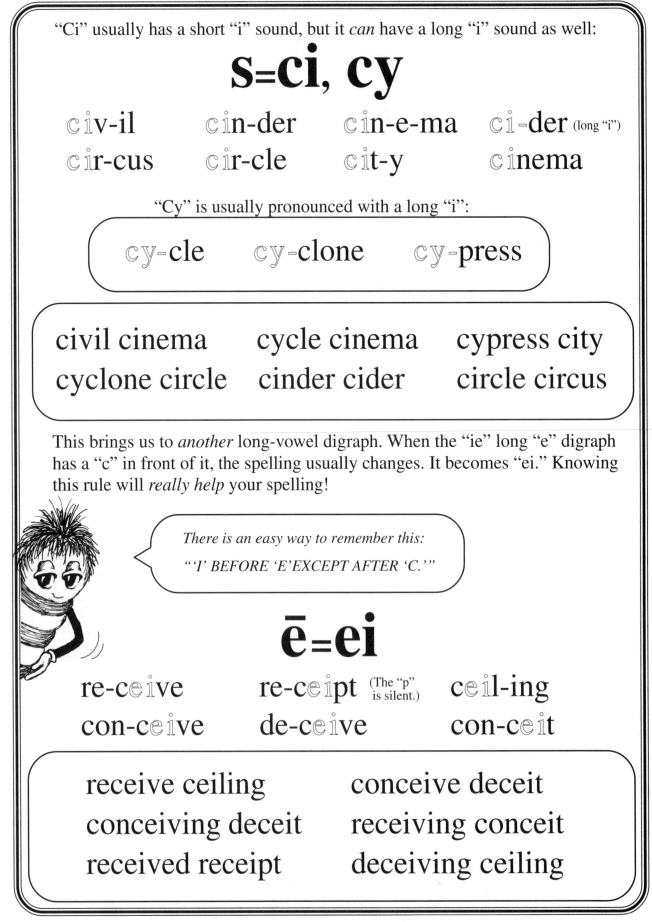

There is an easy way to remember this:
"'I' BEFORE 'E' EXCEPT AFTER 'C.'"

ē=ei

re-ceive	re-ceipt (The "p" is silent.)	ceil-ing
con-ceive	de-ceive	con-ceit

receive ceiling   conceive deceit
conceiving deceit   receiving conceit
received receipt   deceiving ceiling

To BREAK a bad habit...   *...D R O P I T!*

Grace receive	Grace will receive a price of ten cents for that nice lace.
horse prances	The black horse prances and dances in his center cell.
races receive	Gus races to receive his cider, rice, celery, and mince pie.
cycle cinema	Let us cycle to the cinema and see a circus film twice!
cyclone ceiling	Since the cyclone hit, it left a center space in the ceiling.
prince circled	The prince circled the dance twice to be with Grace.
cypress circle	Big old cypress trees circle that nice place in the city.
cel-e-brate spiced	Shall we celebrate with spiced cider at a fancy dance?

BAD HABIT

So far we have learned about digraphs (two letters that make one sound). Now we shall learn about DIPHTHONGS. A diphthong is two vowels that make *two* sounds, but these sounds blend and slide together continuously and are treated as one, in the same syllable.

There are *two* spelling patterns to the "oi" sound: "oi" and "oy." The diacritical mark for this sound is "oi." Read down each column:

oi=oi

(This sound is usually spelled "oi" when it is in the middle of a word.)

oil	void	moist	coin
boil	avoid	hoist	loin
toil	noise	foist	join
foil	noisy	poise	joint
soil	broil	voice	point
coil	spoil	choice	oint-ment
poi-son	tin-foil	re-joice	ap-point-ment

Remember to read the longer words by syllables, covering up part of the word first if you need to (see page 56).
Or, simply put your finger under each syllable as you read it!

(Lessons are a little bit harder now, aren't they? Think of this: EVERYTHING is difficult before it is EASY!)

moist soil	boil oil	noise spoil
boil ointment	avoid poison	join tabloid
choice coin	voice rejoice	point coil
appointment	broil tinfoil	noisy voice
rejoice toil	spoil loin	point choice

oi=oy

(Sometimes this sound is spelled "oy" in the middle of a word, but it is *always* spelled "oy" at the *end* of a word.)

boy	soy	en-joy	Roy
Joyce	des-troy	con-voy	an-noy
toy	oys-ter	joy-ful	em-ploy

---

enjoy soy	joyful Roy	boy enjoys
toy oyster	annoy Joyce	employ Joy
boys annoy	destroy convoy	enjoy oyster

"OI=OI, OY" REVIEW

moist tinfoil	The boy broils his moist fish in tinfoil and enjoys it.
Joyce joining	Joyce enjoys joining Roy to play with his toy coins.
noisy annoys	The boy's noisy voice annoys Joyce and spoils her nap.
spoiled oyster	Roy's spoiled, green oyster is poison. Avoid it!
enjoy boiled	Gus and Joy enjoy boiled eggs in soy oil.

Never FLY into a RAGE unless you are prepared for a ROUGH LANDING...

There are also two spelling patterns for the "ou" sound: "ou" and "ow."
The diacritical mark for this sound is "ou." Read down each column:

ou=ou

(This sound is usually spelled "ou" at the beginning or in the middle of a word.)

out	ouch	bound	house
scout	couch	a-bound	mouse
trout	pouch	pound	douse
shout	crouch	sound	blouse
spout	grouch	found	our
loud	proud	mound	sour
cloud	hound	round	flour
slouch	mount	a-round	foul
mouth	count	ground	bout
boun-ty	ac-count	as-tound	a-bout

Failure is not defeat unless you STOP TRYING...
Kites rise AGAINST the wind, not WITH it!

Read across:

shout ouch	our hound	loud sound
round ground	sour flour	scout about
hound crouch	lout slouch	found pouch
proud mount	douse trout	cloud wound
mouth sound	mouse house	around mound

ou=ow

(This sound is always spelled "ow" when it occurs at the end of a word. It is also found in the middle of words that have multisyllables, or end in "l" or "n.")

Read down each column:

how	town	tow-er	owl
cow	gown	pow-er	fowl
now	down	cow-er	howl
vow	frown	flow-er	jowl
wow	crown	show-er	growl
pow	drown	glow-er	yowl
bow	brown	chow-der	scowl
vow-el	clown	pow-der	prowl
tow-el	crowd	browse	how-dy

If you don't learn to laugh at trouble NOW, you won't have ANYTHING to laugh at when you GROW OLD!

owl frown	bow down	down tower
prowl town	growl yowl	power vowel
how brown	fowl drown	flower power
brown gown	cower down	howdy crowd
clown howl	brown crown	shower towel
yowl scowl	crowd browse	cow chowder

found tower	proud scout	town house
mouse growl	joyful choice	found towel
brown trout	moist oyster	round flower
avoid boy	noisy crowd	hound howl
frown ouch	shout howdy	annoy Joyce

oysters boiled — Gus found moist oysters and boiled them in brown oil.

ointment joint — Rub ointment on the cow's sore joint to avoid a boil.

joyful hound — The joyful hound found a toy mouse in Roy's house.

count brown — Did you count the brown, round trout in our lake?

proud scouts — How proud our Roy is now at joining Boy Scouts!

frown-ing growl-ing — Avoid that noisy, shouting, frowning, growling crowd!

Many a man's TONGUE broke his NOSE!

The "j" sound at the end of a word usually is spelled "-ge." It is spelled "gi," "ge," or "gy" in the beginning or middle of a word.

j=ge, gi, gy

age	rage	cage	page
sage	wage	stage	huge
range	hinge	lunge	large
change	fringe	plunge	gy-rate
frig-id	dan-ger	o-rig-i-nal	Marge

lunge cage	fringe stage	huge wage
Marge rage	hinge barge	large range
danger change	plunge stage	original page

change original — Please change the old original hinge on Marge's range.

plunge danger — The huge cats plunge and gyrate in rage. They smell danger!

Marge wage — Marge, please change my wage, and make it large.

lunge frigid — They lunge in rage in the huge cage on the frigid barge.

The only GOOD LUCK that many great people had was the determination to overcome BAD LUCK!

However, to make the "j" sound at the end of a *short-vowel* word we must add a "d" before the "-ge." We need a double-consonant in order to keep the short-vowel sound.

-j=-dge

edge	fudge	Madge	lodge
hedge	pudg-y	badge	dodge
ledge	budge	badg-er	sludge
wedge	judge	ridge	trudge
pledge	nudge	ledg-er	smudge

edge ledge	Madge budge	judge lodge
pledge badge	smudge fudge	dodge ledge
hodge-podge	pudgy Madge	hedge wedge

edge ledge	They trudge to the edge of the ledge on the ridge.
Madge dodges	Madge dodges the huge badger by the edge of the hedge.
pudgy fudge	Pudgy Gus gobbles huge wedges of fudge in the lodge.
hodge-podge	His room is a hodgepodge of sludge. He pledges to clean it.

A winner LISTENS…a loser just waits until it is HIS turn to TALK!

Madge charge	Madge and Marge charge up the edge of the ridge.
plunges large	Madge plunges off the large bridge near the lodge.
trudges lodge	Pudgy Gus trudges to the lodge for a huge plate of fudge.
badger gyrates	The badger gyrates and wedges himself under the stage.
Marge pledges	Marge pledges that she will not judge the change in Madge.
dodges ridge	Sage dodges the ridge and edges away from the barge.
huge smudge	There is a huge smudge of fudge on the edge of Gus' page.
danger edge	The large badgers smell danger by the edge of the hedge.

Make your life a LIGHT to OTHERS...
A candle loses nothing of its light
by lighting another candle.
Brighten the corner where YOU are!

When we add a suffix beginning with a vowel (such as "-es," "-ed," "-er," or "-est") to words ending in "-y," we must first change the "y" to "i," and then add the suffix. Exception: We *keep* the "y" before adding "-ing." Read across:

-y, -ie

try	tries	tried	try-ing
dry	dries	dried	dry-ing
spy	spies	spied	spy-ing
cry	cries	cried	cry-ing
re-ply	re-plies	re-plied	re-ply-ing
de-ny	de-nies	de-nied	de-ny-ing
stud-y	stud-ies	stud-ied	stud-y-ing
car-ry	car-ries	car-ried	car-ry-ing

silly	silli-er	silli-est
funny	funni-er	funni-est
misty	misti-er	misti-est
bumpy	bumpi-er	bumpi-est
early	earli-er	earli-est

When a word ENDS with "-ie," we drop the final "e," and then add the suffix.
Exception: We change the "ie" to "y" before adding "-ing."

lie	lies	lied	ly-ing
tie	ties	tied	ty-ing
die	dies	died	dy-ing

-f=-ves

To make words ending in "-f" plural, we must first change the "f" to a "v," and then add "-es." Read across the page:

loaf	loaves	wife	wives
leaf	leaves	elf	elves
life	lives	shelf	shelves
thief	thieves	wolf	wolves
be-lief	be-lieves	re-lief	re-lieves

"-Y, -IE" PLUS SUFFIXES AND "-F=-VES" REVIEW

funny crying	funniest cry
drying babies	dried baby
earliest leaf	early leaves
wife crying	wives cried
wolf carries	wolves carry
reply believing	replying belief
denied reply	denying replies
trying study	tried studying
elf believes	elves believed
wolf dying	wolves died
loaf drying	loaves dried
thief lying	thieves lied

FEAR is the darkroom where NEGATIVES are developed...

wolves carried	The huge wolves carried the five crying cubs down the hill.
wives believe	The wives believe that the tiniest babies are lying asleep.
replied loaves	He replied, "Gus denied eating ten loaves of fried cake."
tried spying	Gus tried spying on elves flying in the earliest, mistiest leaves.
cried studying	They cried and tried studying for the earliest test.
believe funnier	I tried to believe that the old joke can get funnier and funnier.
tried replying	He tried replying that his shelves seemed the bumpiest.

It's NOT how hard you FALL,

it's how HIGH

you BOUNCE!

So far, we have learned digraphs that have *long-vowel* sounds, as in "ōo" in "food" which has a long "u" sound (page 165). Now let's learn *another* sound that "oo" makes: "ŏo" as in "foot." Read across the page, and consider using some of the games and activities beginning on page 250 to reinforce the lessons.

ŎO=OO

look	cook	cook-ie	cook-ies
good	wood-en	hood	stood
book	brook	took	nook
shook	soot	wool	hook
woof	roof	foot	foot-step

---

sooty cookie	good book	took hood
stood brook	wood foot	woof woof
wool hook	footstep	shook hoof
crooked book	hook foot	look cookies

---

look sooty	Look at that sooty wooden roof!
stood brook	We stood in the brook and shook.
good cookies	Look, Gus took ten good cookies!
cookbooks	Good cooks look at good cookbooks.

Courage

We CAN'T LEARN how to be BRAVE if we've only had WONDERFUL THINGS happen to us!

ŏŏ d=ould

"Ould" is not really a digraph, but it has the same sound as the digraph we have just learned, "ŏŏ." There are only a few words with this combination:

> could   would   should

ŏŏ =u

There also are a small group of words in which "u" has this sound as well. When reading books later, if you are not sure what sound the "u" makes in a word, try reading it with both the short "u" sound and the "ŏŏ" sound. You will soon see which fits! Read across the page:

pull	full	bull	bul-let
push	push-y	bush	bush-y
put	put-ting	pud-ding	pul-ling

"ŏŏ=OO, OULD, U" REVIEW

could put	should push	full bush
bushy hoof	would pull	put pudding
would push	bull could	bullet could
full bush	pushy bull	pulling bull
could push	should put	full pudding
would look	brook could	should cook
bullet shook	foot would	roof should

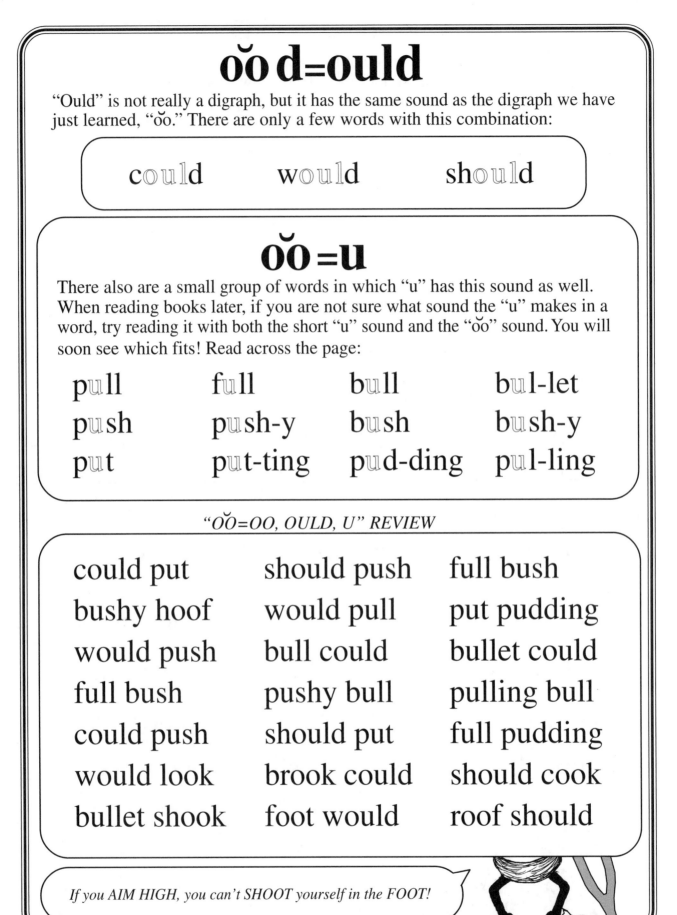

If you AIM HIGH, you can't SHOOT yourself in the FOOT!

would cook   He would cook if he could just
                find a good cookbook.

stood putting I stood and shook, putting one foot
                in the brook near the woods.

should look   I should look at that good book.
                Would you put it down?

took pudding   Gus took a good cookbook and
                cooked a pot full of pudding.

could push   We could put a hook on the hood,
                and push and pull it.

stood wooden   The good pup stood in the bushes
                on a wooden box. Woof!

pushed sooty   He pushed the sooty bull's hoof.
                It stood and looked mad.

look wool   Look, this wool is full of hooks!

SAY what you MEAN,
    and MEAN what you SAY...
        But DON'T say it MEAN!

Note the diacritical mark for this sound. Try looking up one of these words in the dictionary. "Haul," for example, is shown as "hôl." Read down each group of words:

Ô=au

| Paul | pause | sauce | Maude |
| haul | cause | fault | clause |

| Paul pause | haul sauce | cause Maude |
| Maude fault | pause clause | Paul sauce |

Ô=aw

(This sound is spelled "aw" when it occurs at the *end* of a word.)

saw	jaw	dawn	thaw
law	paw	yawn	crawl
hawk	draw	lawn	shawl

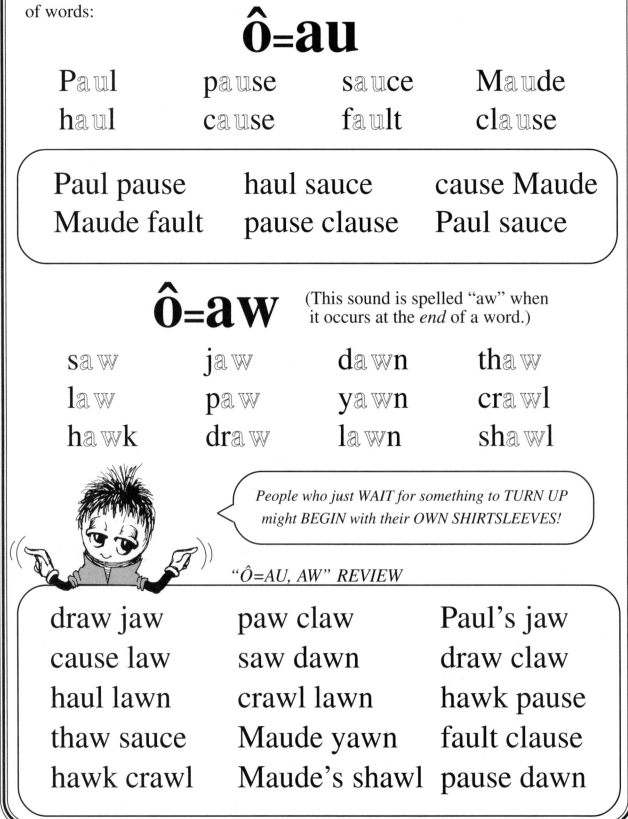

People who just WAIT for something to TURN UP might BEGIN with their OWN SHIRTSLEEVES!

"Ô=AU, AW" REVIEW

draw jaw	paw claw	Paul's jaw
cause law	saw dawn	draw claw
haul lawn	crawl lawn	hawk pause
thaw sauce	Maude yawn	fault clause
hawk crawl	Maude's shawl	pause dawn

ôl=al

Read across the page:

halt	hal-ter	false	fal-ter
al-so	al-most	al-ways	salt
al-ter	al-ter-nate	bald	scald

alter salt	almost bald	also scald
also halt	almost halt	always halt
always falter	false halter	also alternate

(The "ôl" sound is spelled "-all" at the *end* of a word.)

ôl=all

all	wall	mall	fall
tall	stall	call	call-ing
hall	ball	small	small-er

"ÔL=AL , ALL" REVIEW

tall hall	all bald	alter ball
also fall	small wall	false salt
scald ball	falter stall	also small
almost tall	always halt	small halter

It's nice to know that when you HELP someone up a HILL you're a little nearer the top YOURSELF!

Ô=O

"O" is not a digraph, but in a number of words the "o" has the "ô" sound instead of "ŏ." The sounds are very similar, but the name of something to eat will quickly show you the difference: hŏt dôg

When reading books, if you are not sure which sound the word has, try both. *One* will fit! Read across the page:

dog	hog	fog	log
clog	smog	frog	lost
boss	cost	off	of-fer
soft	loft	floss	cross
moss	loss	toss	frost

"Ô=AU, AW, AL, ALL, O" REVIEW

salt hog	dog paw	Paul tall
crawl fog	hog sauce	call dog
tall hawk	lawn cost	call boss
also offer	cross lawn	all sauce
frog yawn	frost thaw	crawl loft
dog halter	false dawn	lost shawl
toss floss	almost clog	saw smog
soft dawn	Maude cross	moss lawn
small frog	always yawn	small fault

Hardening of the HEART ages people more quickly than hardening of the ARTERIES…

"Ô=AU, AW, AL, ALL, O" REVIEW

small yawns   His small pup yawns and crawls on his paws to the ball.

hawk almost   We saw the small hawk almost fall on the frosty lawn.

cross offered   Gus felt cross when he saw all the roast hog offered for dinner.

all halted   They all halted and saw the soft pink dawn cross the sky.

frog draw   I saw a small frog I could almost draw, and also a dog.

always halts   Paul always halts and crawls on the tall, mossy log in the fog.

Maude soft   Maude offers almost all her cash for the small, soft dog.

Paul floss   Paul did not always floss, and he lost almost all his teeth.

So far we have had words with double-consonant beginnings, as in "trip." Now let's read words with *three-letter* consonant beginnings. Read down each group:

rip	ray	ream	ice
trip	pray	cream	rice
strip	spray	scream	thrice
rain	rap	lat-ter	ash
train	trap	plat-ter	rash
strain	strap	splat-ter	thrash
ripe	ray	ram	roll
tripe	tray	cram	troll
stripe	stray	scram	stroll

The *first* word is also part of the *second* word in each phrase below. (However, they have different meanings.) Read across the page:

at splat	rap scrap	lit split
ill thrill	raw straw	rub scrub
lint splint	lash splash	rice thrice
ape scrape	row throw	retch stretch
ink sprinkle	ring string	lend splendid
ream stream	rush thrush	ram scramble

We make a LIVING by what we GET…
But we make a LIFE by what we GIVE!

Practice a group of these words at a time, reading down. Then read them *across!*
(It's fun to use these words with one of the activities or games in the appendix!)

thr-	str-	scr-	spl-
thrill	strip	scrap	split
threw	straw	scratch	splat
three	street	scream	splash
throat	string	scrub	splint
thrash	strap	scrape	splin-ter
thrush	stream	screen	splat-ter
thrown	strong	scruff	sprin-kle
throw	stroke	scram-ble	splen-did
thrice	stretch	scruffy	splay
thread	strange	Scrooge	splutter

All of these words contain *short vowels*. Read down, then across:

strap	scrap	thrash	splat
strip	scrub	throb	split
struck	scratch	thrill	splen-did

All of these words contain *long vowels*. Read down, then across:

stray	scrape	three	thrice
street	screen	throw	spray
strike	scream	threw	stroke

The words in these phrases begin with the *same* three-letter consonant blend:

three thrush	strip string	straw strap
throat thrill	threw three	split spleen
split splinter	stroll street	spring sprint
throw thrash	strain strap	scrimp scrap
strong stroke	stripe strife	stream stretch
splatter splint	scrub scrape	splendid splash
scratch scream	scruffy screen	scramble scream

The words in these phrases begin with *different* three-letter blends:

scrub strip	throw splat	three strikes
straw string	spray street	scrap Scrooge
stroke throat	three splints	stretch thread
thrush splash	threw screen	splendid street
splatter stream	scroll scrape	scratchy throat
sprinkle splatter	strong splinter	scruffy spread
strip sprinkler	strain scramble	spring thrush
strange script	throw strike	thrifty scrap

The GREATEST IGNORANCE is to reject something you know NOTHING ABOUT!

THREE-CONSONANT BEGINNINGS REVIEW

Read as many of these sentences as you can. It may take several lessons to read them all—just read what you can, and save the rest for another day.

(And remember: Try to incorporate some of the activities and games beginning on page 250 when doing these lessons, These words can be difficult to read, and making a game out of it makes it more fun and helps take the pressure off as well!)

splashes splatters — The rain splashes and splatters as it strikes the strong screen.

scrapes splendid — Gus scrapes and scrubs the splendid cream on his plate.

three strange — Three strange flies thrash and strain in the strong bug strip.

stream splashes — The stream splashes and sprays my three backpack straps.

splendid thrush — We scramble and strain to stroke the splendid spring thrush.

thrashed strikes — The boy screamed and thrashed as he threw three strikes!

scratched scraped — She scratched and scraped her splinter, and it throbbed.

scrambles strains — Gus scrambles and strains as he strolls up the scruffy street.

Life is more FUN when you DON'T KEEP SCORE!

ĕ=ea

On page 97 we learned that the digraph "ea" has the long "e" sound.
Sometimes it can have a short "e" sound as well. Read across the page:

dead	read	bread
breath	deaf	head
heav-y	stead-y	read-y
weath-er	leath-er	feath-er
heav-en	leav-en	sweat-er
wealth	health	in-stead

ĕ=ai

In a few words, "ai" can have a short "e" sound also. Read down the page:

a-gain

said

foun-tain

a-gainst

moun-tain

OPTIMISM is that cheerful frame of mind
that enables a TEA KETTLE to SING
even though it's in HOT WATER up to its NOSE!

ready again	said deaf
breath said	health bread
wealth again	feather head
heavy leather	leaven bread
health instead	heavy sweater
against mountain	steady fountain
heav-en-ly weather	mountain weather

We have already learned that "y" sounds like long "e" when added to the end of a word. In the middle of a word, "y" usually has a short "i" sound.

ĭ =

Read across the page:

myth	gym	sym-bol
lyr-ic	crys-tal	cyn-ic
syr-up	typ-i-cal	sys-tem
Lynn	hymn (The "n" is silent.)	mys-ter-y
Flynn	hys-ter-ic-al	Syl-vi-a
syn-thet-ic	hyp-no-sis	sym-pa-thy

ĭ = ui

In a few words, "ui" can have a short "i" sound also. Read across:

build	built	builder
guild	guilt	guilty

guilty Lynn	typical builder
Flynn builds	Sylvia's guild
lyr-i-cal hymn	build-ing gym
crystal building	built cyl-in-der
synthetic syrup	sym-bol-ic myth
gym-nast guilty	hypnosis system
sym-pa-thet-ic Lynn	hys-ter-i-cal cynic

Even if you're on the RIGHT TRACK you'll get RUN OVER if you just SIT there!

Phonics Pathways: Clear Steps to Easy Reading and Perfect Spelling

A few "a" words sound like ŏ. **Ŏ=a** Read across the page:

wand	wander	wasp
want	wanted	wanting
father	wanton	Wanda

Wanda wants   father wanders

"Ă=EA, AI"; "Ĭ=Y, UI"; AND "Ŏ=A" REVIEW

Wanda read	deaf wasp
health system	Lynn wants
wants syrup	father builds
already guilty	Flynn read
heavy crystal	want leather
read mystery	crystal wand
steady fountain	wanton cynic
heav-en-ly hymn	symbol wealth
gymnast wanders	Cyril's sweater
mountain weather	typical builder
wants sym-pa-thy	Sylvia's feather
Wanda hys-ter-i-cal	wander mountain

More people RUST OUT than WEAR OUT...

ŭ=o

At times "o" is pronounced with a short "u" sound. These words frequently have "m" or "n" next to them. Read across the page:

won	son	from	done
none	ton	mon-ey	some
lov-er	cov-er	a-bove	a-mong
shove	glove	com-fort	hon-ey
oth-er	moth-er	broth-er	a-noth-er
mon-key	don-key	noth-ing	Mon-day

one (wŭn)   once (wŭns)   of (ŭv)

ŭ=ou

In a few words, "ou" sounds like "ŭ":

touch	young	cous-in
couple	double	coun-try

Sometimes even "oo" and "a" have a short "u" sound!

ŭ=oo   ŭ=a

flood   blood   was (wuz)

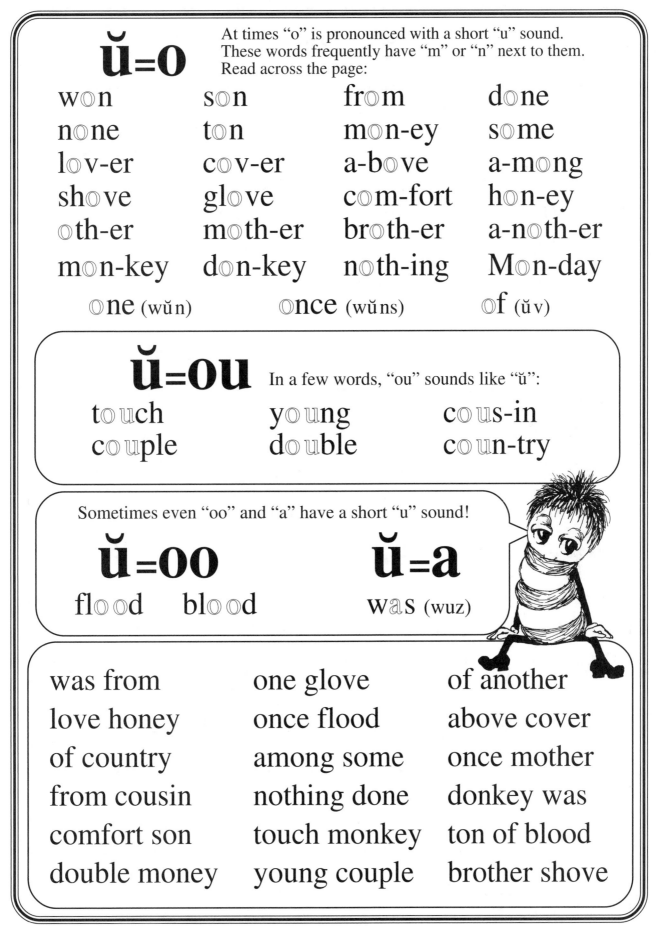

---

was from	one glove	of another
love honey	once flood	above cover
of country	among some	once mother
from cousin	nothing done	donkey was
comfort son	touch monkey	ton of blood
double money	young couple	brother shove

ŭ = ə

In multisyllable words, the unaccented vowel sound (including vowel digraphs) often resembles a short "u" sound. The diacritical mark for this sound is "ə." It is called a "schwa," a German word that means silence instead of a vowel sound. It isn't really silent, but is indefinite and neutral in sound. It certainly makes spelling a lot more complicated, since the schwa sound can represent *any one* of the vowels! N O T E: In all of the words listed on this page, the schwa sounds are highlighted. (You may prefer to just read these words for now, and learn to spell them later.)

so´-fa	(a=ə)	so´-fŭ
spo´-ken	(e=ə)	spo´-kŭn
san´-ity	(i=ə)	san´-ŭ-ty
gal´-lop	(o=ə)	gal´-lŭ-p
fo´-cus	(u=ə)	fo´-cŭs

Many words beginning or ending with an unaccented "a" have the schwa sound:

a-rise´	a-woke´	a-lone´	a-way´
a-while´	a-void´	a-round´	a-cross´
at-tack´	at-tain´	at-tend´	at-tach´
tu´-ba	dra´-ma	ex´-tra	so´-fa
so´-da	chi´-na	ze´-bra	del´-ta
for´-mu-la	ba-nan´-a	um-brel´-la	va-nil´-la

We also see it frequently with ending syllables, but the schwa can occur anywhere:

se´-cond	spi´-nal	dir-ect´	lem´-on
se´-rum	lov´-a-ble	les´-son	man´-age
cho´-sen	meth´-od	ve-loc´-i-ty	de-vel´-op

An APOLOGY is a GOOD WAY to have the LAST WORD...

glove another   Bud lost his glove but got
                    another one from Mom.

double banana   Gus just loves to munch a
                    double banana nut soda.

nothing done   Nothing was done to stop
                    the flood from coming.

monkey shoved   One month a young monkey
                    shoved my brother.

once blood   Once some blood was taken
                    from my other son.

loved touch   Mother loved to touch the
                    fat, young, fluffy puppy.

*Problems can be OBSTACLES
or STEPPING STONES,*

depending upon how we see them…

*(Obstacles are those depressing things
we see whenever we stop looking
at our goals.)*

This sentence uses all short "u" spelling patterns. Copy it, and circle these sounds.
Then write your *own* sentence, using as many of these spelling patterns as you can
think of:

Once his young pup was running from a flood.

The words in these phrases each have the *same* short-vowel sound. Read across:

one ton	built gym
want father	double cover
won money	young couple
steady head	another flood
comfort son	country cousin

The words in these phrases each have a *different* short-vowel sound. Read across:

once again	father ready
cover syrup	Lynn's cousin
build above	another hymn
steady couple	Monday again
touch crystal	wants mystery
typical father	wander mountain

father crystal   Lynn's father built another heavy crystal fountain in the country.

steady builds   Steady rain builds another flood in typical mountain weather.

again cover   Once again, it comforts Gus to cover banana nut bread with tons and tons and *tons* of honey syrup!

LEARN from the mistakes of OTHERS...
For nobody can ever LIVE long enough to make them all HIMSELF!

CONTRACTIONS

Here is an introduction to contractions. A CONTRACTION is what happens when *two words* are run together to make *one word*, and *one or more letters are removed* from the second word. An APOSTROPHE is substituted for the missing letter(s). We use contractions as *shortcuts* when reading or speaking. Here is an example:

> I am = Iam = I̶am = I'm

is = 's

she is = she's

he is = he's

it is = it's

are = 're

we are = we're

they are = they're

you are = you're

will = 'll

I will = I'll

he will = he'll

she will = she'll

we will = we'll

it will = it'll

you will = you'll

they will = they'll

not = n't

is not = isn't

are not = aren't

do not = don't

(dŭz) does not = doesn't

did not = didn't

can not = can't

could not = couldn't

was not = wasn't

were not = weren't

(hăv) have not = haven't

has not = hasn't

had not = hadn't

should not = shouldn't

would not = wouldn't

CONTRACTIONS REVIEW

Read and write each sentence. Then name the *original words* in each contraction:

It's raining.

You haven't eaten.

You're limping.

She'll eat later.

I wasn't kidding.

Isn't Gus funny?

I don't have it.

He can't swim yet.

Shouldn't we go?

He didn't sing well.

We're eating lunch.

He'll be careful.

They'll come soon.

They're running.

He's running very fast!

We aren't afraid.

They weren't asleep.

She doesn't think so.

I wouldn't trust him.

They couldn't sleep.

We'll move soon.

It'll be fine.

She's sick.

I'm going.

The windmill is moved BY its surroundings,
but the electric fan MOVES its surroundings...
WHICH ONE ARE YOU?

We have had a few silent letters so far, like the "magic e," "-ce," and "-ould." Here are some more. When a multi-syllable word ends in unaccented "-le," the "e" is silent. On page 106 we learned that consonant endings on short-vowel words must be doubled before adding other endings. This is true for "-le" endings as well. Also, note how "-le" words are divided: except for "-ckle," the letter *before* the "-le" ending is kept *with* the "-le." Read down each group:

-ckle

tick-le
pick-le
cack-le
crack-le

-ple

sim-ple
sam-ple
dim-ple
pim-ple
top-ple
ap-ple

-fle

raf-fle
ruf-fle
muf-fle
shuf-fle

-gle

an-gle
tan-gle
bun-gle
jun-gle
jan-gle
jin-gle
tin-gle
sin-gle

-dle

sad-dle
pad-dle
han-dle
can-dle
mid-dle
mud-dle
noo-dle
poo-dle

-ble

gob-ble
hob-ble
bab-ble
dab-ble
bum-ble
rum-ble
tum-ble
crum-ble
grum-ble
a-ble
ta-ble
ca-ble
fee-ble
bub-ble
dou-ble
trou-ble
ter-ri-ble
hor-ri-ble

-tle

tat-tle
cat-tle
lit-tle
brit-tle
ket-tle

-zle

siz-zle
fiz-zle
raz-zle
daz-zle
nuz-zle
puz-zle
guz-zle

The LESS you talk, the MORE you are listened to!

"-LE" REVIEW

The words in these phrases are the *same* except for the beginning letters:

razzle dazzle	tickle pickle	huddle cuddle
apple dapple	cattle tattle	simple dimple
feeble steeple	jingle jangle	middle riddle
sizzle fizzle	poodle noodle	double trouble
snuffle truffle	muddle puddle	mumble grumble

The words in these phrases are all *different*, and have different beginning letters:

shuffle table	gobble apple	humble Mable
kettle jingle	cattle hobble	little apple
double ruffle	tickle poodle	nibble truffle
puzzle tangle	jungle muddle	sample pickle
terrible trouble	horrible rumble	poodle puddle

tickle cuddle	Gus likes to tickle and cuddle his simple little poodle.
middle muddle	I'm in the middle of a muddle as I fumble with this puzzle!
snuffles truffles	Gus snuffles truffles and his poodle nibbles noodles.
kettle sizzles	The little kettle sizzles, fizzles, and bubbles on the table.

NOBODY ever left footprints in the sands of time by SITTING DOWN!

Silent letters can be difficult to learn. This section also may be more difficult because the words are not sounded out. Therefore, some of the more difficult words are shown also to add to those of you who might find it helpful.

19000

knot	knob	knelt
knit	knit-ted	knit-ting
knock	knack	knuck-le
knife	know	known
knee	kneel	kneel-ing

w

wrist	wrap	wreck
wring	wrong	wrung
write	wreath	wrote

l

talk (tôk)	walk (wôk)	stalk (stôk)
half (hăf)	calf (kăf)	chalk (chôk)

knock wrist	knee kneel	stalk calf
wrong knee	knock chalk	write half
half wrong	wrote talk	calf kneel
wrap knife	knelt wreck	know walk
knitted wrap	know knack	wrong knob
wring knuckle	wrap wreath	known knot

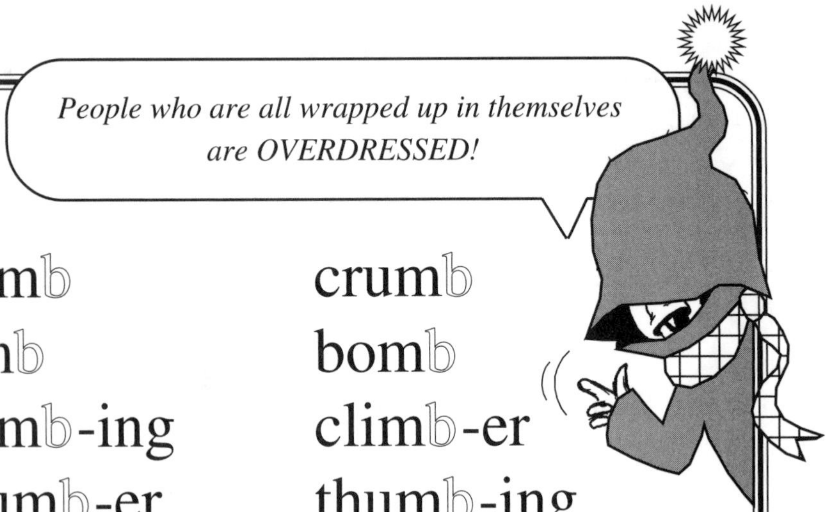
People who are all wrapped up in themselves are OVERDRESSED!

b

dumb	numb	crumb
lamb	limb	bomb
climb	climb-ing	climb-er
comb	plumb-er	thumb-ing

t

of-ten (ôfən)	sof-ten (sôfən)	lis-ten (lĭsən)
nes-tle (nĕsəl)	wres-tle (rĕsəl)	wres-tling
lis-ten-ing	glis-ten (glĭsən)	cas-tle (kăsəl)
has-ten (hāsən)	chas-ten (chāsən)	whis-tle (wĭsəl)

h

hour (our)	hour-ly	ghet-to (gĕtō)
honest (ŏnəst)	hon-est-ly	hon-or (ŏnər)
ghost (gōst)	ghast-ly (găstlē)	ghoul (go͞ol)

listen often	castle nestle	climb limb
lamb glisten	ghastly climb	listen ghetto
wrestle crumb	numb thumb	lamb nestle
often wrestle	dumb ghost	hourly climb
soften thumb	listen whistle	honest honor
plumber hasten	climbing limb	ghastly bomb

dumb lamb   The dumb lamb knows how to
                  climb in my lap and nestle.

often talk   They often talk and whistle as
                  they hasten up the peaks.

thumb knife   Gus cut his thumb with a knife
                  when he ate half of the calf.

plumber knows   The plumber knows our sink
                  well. Honestly, it is a wreck!

walk castle   We often walk to the castle
                  and listen to the hourly talk.

kneels knocks   She kneels and knocks half of
                  the knitting from her wrist.

knows knees   She knows how to walk on her
                  knees and her thumbs.

honestly wrong   Honestly, this is the wrong
                  walk. We must hasten home.

A mind stretched to a **NEW IDEA**
never goes back to its original dimension!

There are three main patterns to silent "gh": "igh," "ough," and "augh." (Remember to put a piece of paper underneath the line you are reading if it makes it easier for you, or just move your finger underneath each word.) Read across the page:

ī=igh

sigh	sight	plight
fight	flight	fright
tight	right	might
light	slight	bright
night	high	thigh

Each of us is born with TWO ENDS...
one to SIT ON, and one to THINK WITH.
SUCCESS depends upon which one we use the most...

HEADS we WIN...
TAILS we LOSE!

light night	right flight	thigh high
might sigh	night fright	tight fight
right thigh	night light	slight sigh
might light	high flight	right sight
slight fight	bright light	sigh plight
fright sight	night flight	sight light

ô=ough, augh

ought	fought	bought
thought	sought	brought

caught	taught	daugh-ter
slaugh-ter	haugh-ty	fraught
naugh-ty	naugh-tier	naugh-tiest

ō=ough

though	al-though
dough	thor-ough

Some people are a lot like BOATS...
They TOOT LOUDEST when they're in a FOG!

crawl caught	Paul ought
fought cause	caught paw
brought salt	taught Paul
bought sauce	brought halter
halt slaughter	small daughter
sought dough	almost thought
although naughty	Maude thorough

might though	Gus might take a night flight, though he fights his fright.
brought right	Paul brought the right game. He thought it might be taught.
ought thought	She ought to have thought of her bright daughter.
small daughter	His small daughter might put bright lights on her high tree.
although caught	The thief fought, although he got caught in the night light.
sighed thought	I sighed as I thought of how I sought the right dog.
fight fright-ful	The fight was a frightful sight, and was brought to a halt. Maude was naughty!

A smile is a CURVE

that can set

a lot of things STRAIGHT!

Sometimes "ei" and "eigh" sound like long "a." Read across the page:

ā=ei

vein	veil	skein
feign (silent "g")	rein	rein-deer

ā=eigh

Here is a new verse to the poem we learned on page 170:

> *"I" before "e" except after "c,"*
> *or when sounding like "a"*
> *as in "neighbor" and "weigh."*

eight	eighth	sleigh
weigh	weight	freight
neigh	neigh-ing	weigh-ing
neigh-bor	neigh-bor-ly	neigh-bor-hood

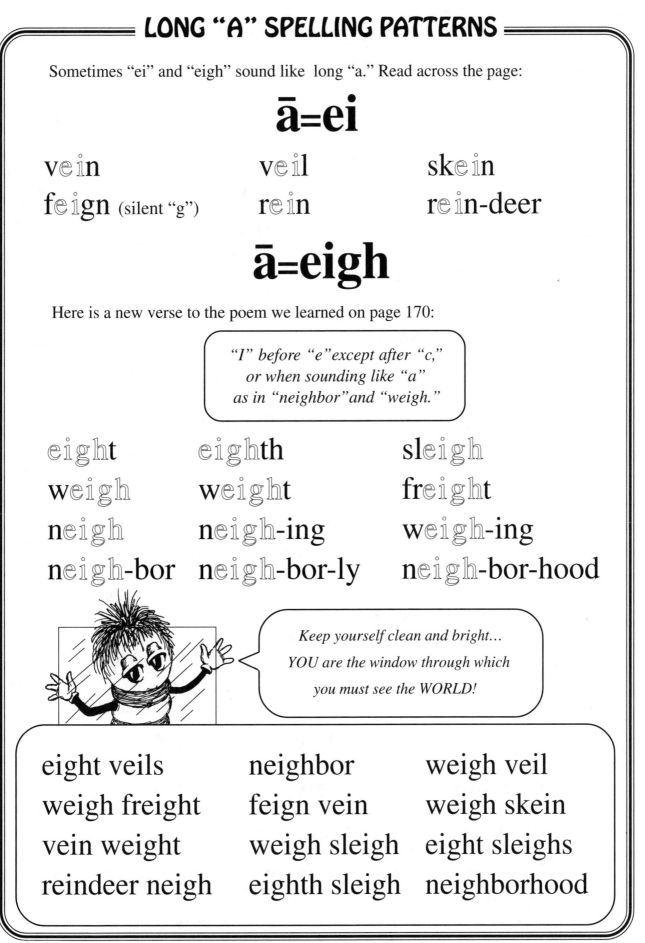

Keep yourself clean and bright…
YOU are the window through which
you must see the WORLD!

eight veils	neighbor	weigh veil
weigh freight	feign vein	weigh skein
vein weight	weigh sleigh	eight sleighs
reindeer neigh	eighth sleigh	neighborhood

There are two more spelling patterns for long "a."
Read down the page:

ā=ey

hey	prey	o-bey
they	grey	sur-vey

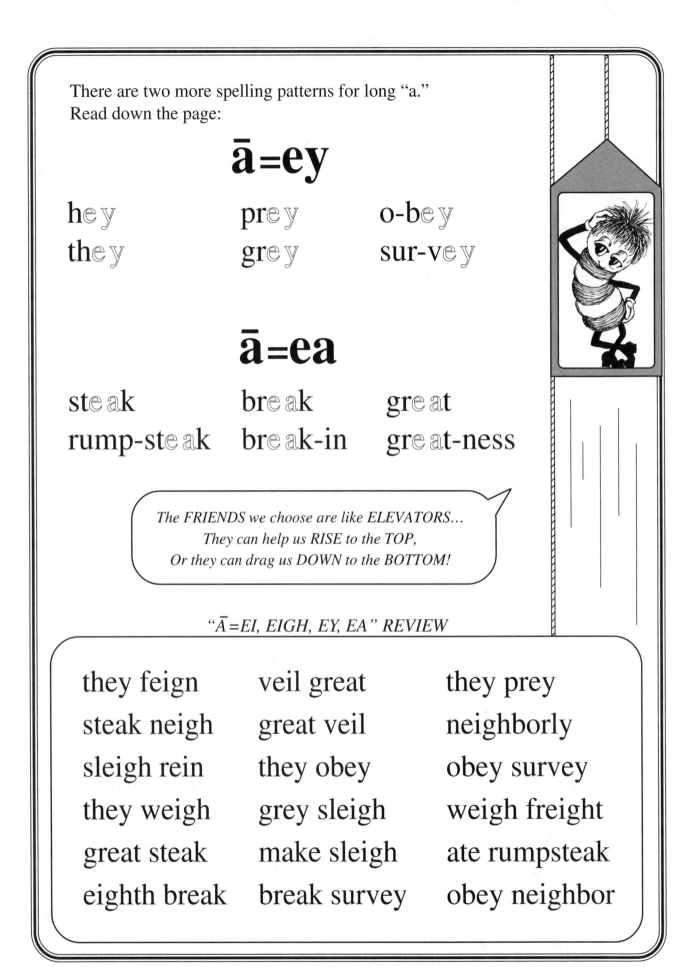

ā=ea

steak	break	great
rump-steak	break-in	great-ness

The FRIENDS we choose are like ELEVATORS…
They can help us RISE to the TOP,
Or they can drag us DOWN to the BOTTOM!

"Ā=EI, EIGH, EY, EA" REVIEW

they feign	veil great	they prey
steak neigh	great veil	neighborly
sleigh rein	they obey	obey survey
they weigh	grey sleigh	weigh freight
great steak	make sleigh	ate rumpsteak
eighth break	break survey	obey neighbor

obeyed eighth

They obeyed and grabbed the eighth rein on the sleigh.

they survey

They survey their prey and think, "Great rumpsteak!"

neighborhood

They wore their great veils in the grey neighborhood.

eight gained

Gus ate eight great steaks, and he gained a lot of weight.

great break

They pray the great doctor will not break eight veins.

they sleigh

They played on a great sleigh pulled by eight tiny reindeer.

neighbors

Eight great neighbors stay to help weigh the freight.

eighteen

They had eighteen grey days of rain in Spain!

Don't just WAIT for opportunity to come knocking at your door…
Go out and FIND it!
If you're looking for a BIG OPPORTUNITY, seek out a BIG PROBLEM…
PROBLEMS are nothing but OPPORTUNITIES IN WORK CLOTHES!

z, zh, sh=s

On page 57 we learned four words in which "s" sounds like "z": "is," "his," "as," and "has." Words ending in "se" can sound like "z" also. Read across the page:

rose	pose	nose
rise	a-rise	wise
ease	tease	please
chose	choose	cheese
use	fuse	re-fuse
pause	clause	be-cause

Here are some words with the "zh" sound: a-zure
plea-sure   mea-sure   trea-sure

And here are two "s" words that sound like *"sh"!*

sure   sugar

please pose	please rise	sugar nose
use treasure	measure nose	sure please
choose sugar	sure-ly please	tease Rose
azure treasure	measure fuse	wise because
chose pleasure	wise pleasure	refuse cheese

The real voyage of discovery consists not of seeking NEW LANDSCAPES, but of having NEW EYES!

pleased treasure	I am pleased beyond measure to win the azure treasure.
surely measure	It's surely not easy to measure the alligator's long nose.
pleasure because	Gus gets pleasure because his nose is in sugar and cheese.
pauses refuses	Rose pauses and wisely refuses to choose the easy path.
chose because	She chose to pause because the azure rose was thorny.
arises pauses	He arises, pauses, and blows his nose. He surely has a cold!
refuses teasing	He refuses to stop teasing Gus. Rose pauses, rises, and says: "Please do not tease Gus *any more!*"

Happiness is not the ABSENCE of conflict, but the ability to COPE with it...
It takes both sunshine AND rain to make a LOVELY RAINBOW!

Read across the page:

f=ph

phone	pho-ny	tel-e-phone
phys-ics	phys-i-cal	Phil-ip
pam-phlet	el-e-phant	phan-tom
phon-ics	or-phan	pho-to-graph
phase	phrase	pho-no-graph

phony phantom	elephant photo
telephone orphan	orphan elephant
physics pamphlet	physical phase
phantom photograph	phonics phrase
Philip's phonograph	Phil's telephone

f=gh

rough (rŭf)	e-nough (enŭf)	tough (tŭf)
laugh (lăf)	laugh-ing	cough (kôf)

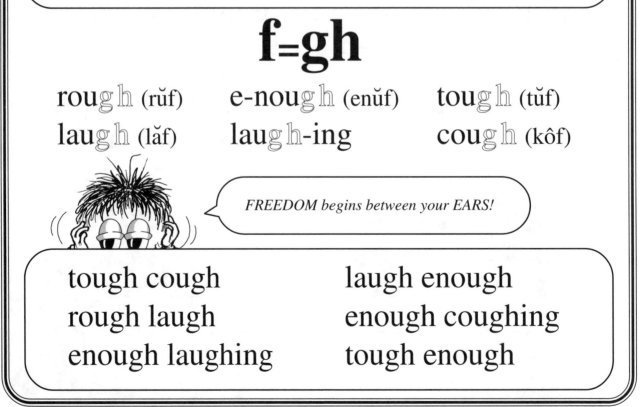

FREEDOM begins between your EARS!

tough cough	laugh enough
rough laugh	enough coughing
enough laughing	tough enough

Read across:

tough physical	tough phrase
elephant cough	rough cough
telephone Phil	phony telephone
Philip laugh	Philip photograph
enough phonics	enough laughter
laughing orphan	laughing elephant

laugh phantom — They laugh and laugh at the phony phantom.

telephone rough — Telephone Phil. He has a rough cough and is in bed.

elephant tough — Be careful! That elephant is tough and rough.

orphan enough — That orphan has had enough rough times. Let's help!

photograph Phil — Photograph Phil and his fancy physics pamphlet.

Phil phonics — Both Phil and Gus have had enough phonics for today.

TRYING TIMES are NOT the times to STOP TRYING!

Sometimes "ch" can sound like "k"! # k=ch Read across the page:

chord	chor-us	ache
chron-ic	chron-i-cle	chem-ist
school	schol-ar	schol-as-tic
Chris-tie	chris-ten	Christ-mas (The "t" is silent.)
scheme	sched-ule	Chris-to-pher

christen Chris	school chronicle
chronic chord	chemist scheme
Christmas chorus	Christie scholar
Christopher ache	scholastic schedule

schedule Christie — Shall we schedule a day to christen baby Christie?

chemist scheme — The chemist has a scheme that cures a chronic cough.

Christopher aches — Christopher aches to sing in the Christmas chorus.

school schedule — Chris has a very long school schedule this year.

ATTITUDE is the mind's PAINTBRUSH... it can COLOR any situation!

ANOTHER "R" MODIFIED VOWEL SOUND:
"ÂR=-ARE, -AIR, -EAR, -ERE, -EIR"

When we add an "e" to a word *ending* in "-ar," making a new word, it results in an *entirely new* "r" modified vowel sound. *The "magic e" strikes again!* It sounds like "air." There are several ways to spell this sound. Read across:

âr=are

fare	care	bare	dare
share	stare	glare	rare
spare	scare	snare	mare
ware	blare	flare	pare

âr=air

air	fair	pair	hair
lair	stair	flair	chair

âr=ear

bear	tear	wear	pear

âr=ere

there (means "direction")   where

ONE MORE word has this sound. It sounds exactly like the word "there," but is SPELLED differently and has a completely different MEANING:

their (*means "belonging to them"*)

Where are their cakes? Over there?

dare bear	fare there	their pair
flair wear	rare pear	snare lair
bare chair	bear stare	stair there
scare bear	share flare	fair Claire
their mare	Mary cares	where hare

share chair	Mary, please share that fair chair over there with Claire.
where hairy	Where is their rare pair of black hairy bears?
stare tear	They dare to stare at the tear in my spare pair of pants.
scary bears	The scary bears glare and stare in their lair under the stairs.
Blair pears	Mary and Blair stare at their fair share of rare pears.
dares wear	Mary dares Gus to wear his pair of rare boots to the fair.

The GREATEST OAK was once a LITTLE NUT that HELD ITS GROUND!

This section deals with some spelling rules that are really useful to know. (They are not necessary to know in order to read, however. You may wish to just read them for now, and learn these rules more thoroughly at a later date.)

Homonyms

Strictly speaking, true *homonyms* have the *same* sound and spelling, but *different meanings*. The meaning needed is determined by the context of the word within the sentence:

I can read well. We can apples in the Fall.

I cannot bear snakes. He saw big bear tracks.

That rose is very red. I rose from my chair.

Homophones

On pages 165 and 166 we learned about words that *sound* the same, as homonyms do but have different *spellings* as well as meanings, such as "too," "to," and "two." (See also "their" and "there" on page 219.) These words are called *homophones*.

Homophones certainly make life complicated when it comes to spelling! The more you read, however, the better able you will be to select the correct spelling when you need to write any of these words.

Write a simple sentence using each of the words listed below. Use the dictionary to find out the meaning of any word you are unsure of:

here hear	to two too	*If you can't get people to listen any other way, tell them it's a SECRET!*
do due	blue blew	
shoo shoe	pane pain	
break brake	steak stake	
no know	great grate	
shone shown	there their	
raise rays	steel steal	
cheep cheap	choose chews	

(SSSSshhhhhhhhhh...)

There are many more. I'll bet *you* can think of some that are not listed here! It's fun to keep a list and see how many you can come up with.

Homographs

Homographs, like homonyms, are words that are spelled the same way and have different meanings. But homographs usually have different *pronunciations* also! As with homonyms, it's easy to determine which meaning we need, just by reading the sentence. This "context clue" will tell us exactly which word fits.

Ben likes to read books.
Ben read a book today.

Learn from the OYSTER...with a LITTLE GRIT he can produce a PEARL!

The actor took a bow at the end of the play.
Katie had a big, fat, pink bow in her hair.

We live in a small, wooden house.
I like to hear a live band best of all!

Gus got a big tear in his best pants.
Jan felt sad and a tear rolled down her cheek.

The dove sang and sang in the big pine tree.
Jan dove in the water but bumped her head.

Gus will lead us to the table with cream cakes.
Gus' tummy feels as heavy as a lump of lead.

HOMONYM, HOMOPHONE, & HOMOGRAPH CHART

	SOUND	SPELLING	MEANING
HOMONYMS	Same	Same	Different
HOMOPHONES	Same	Different	Different
HOMOGRAPHS	Different	Same	Different

MULTI-SYLLABLE WORDS WITH SUFFIXES

On page 68 we learned that when we add a suffix beginning with a vowel to a single-syllable, short-vowel word ending with only *one* consonant, we *double* that consonant before adding the suffix. In a *multi-syllable* short-vowel word, if the accent is on the *last syllable,* we *also* double the last consonant before adding these suffixes, in order to keep the short-vowel sound.

sub-mit´	sub-mit´-ted	sub-mit´-ting
ad-mit	ad-mit-ted	ad-mit-ting
per-mit	per-mit-ted	per-mit-ting
com-pel	com-pel-led	com-pel-ling

If the accent is *not* on the last syllable, we *do not* double the final consonant before adding these suffixes:

mar´-ket	mar´-ket-ed	mar´-ket-ing
vis-it	vis-it-ed	vis-it-ing
trum-pet	trum-pet-ed	trum-pet-ing
hap-pen	hap-pen-ed	hap-pen-ing

It's FUN to mix these words up and try to spell them, because you can figure out the correct spelling by listening VERY CAREFULLY to hear which syllable is ACCENTED. It's like solving a PUZZLE! Try it.

admitted	visited	permitted
submitting	trumpeting	visiting
happened	compelled	marketed
permitting	happening	admitting
submitted	trumpeted	submitting
compelling	marketing	permitting

"-ce, -ge"

When a word ends in "-ce" or "-ge," we keep the "e" before adding "-ous" or "-able." This keeps the "j" sound of "g" and the "s" sound of "c":

out-ra-ge*ous*   gor-ge*ous*   cou-ra-ge*ous*

peace-*able*   change-*able*   trace-*able*
no-tice-*able*   re-place-*able*   dam-age-*able*

-able, -ible

If a word is complete in itself *without* the ending, we usually spell it "-able." If not, most of the time (but not always!) we spell it "-ible":

read-*able*   tax-*able*   crush-*able*
suit-*able*   pack-*able*   pre-fer-*able*
bend-*able*   mend-*able*   pre-vent-*able*

cred-*ible*   vis-*ible*   ed-*ible*
pos-s*ible*   ter-r*ible*   com-pat-*ible*

People are like stained glass windows...
They SPARKLE and SHINE
when the sun is out,
but when the darkness sets in
their TRUE BEAUTY is revealed
ONLY if there is a LIGHT WITHIN!

A PREFIX is a syllable that is attached to the front of a word. Usually this changes its meaning. There are many prefixes, but we shall try just a few, so that you can see what they are.

pre- (means before, or in front of)

| pre-mix | pre-cool | pre-heat |
| pre-judge | pre-ma-ture | pre-pay |

sub- (means under, or beneath)

sub-way	sub-let	sub-ma-rine
sub-di-vide	sub-mit	sub-tract
sub-con-tract	sub-arc-tic	sub-merge

re- (usually means again, back)

re-act	re-do	re-copy
re-cov-er	re-place	re-paint
re-heat	re-fresh	re-turn

auto- (means by oneself, or itself)

| auto-mat | auto-mo-bile | auto-bus |
| auto-mat-ic | auto-mo-tive | auto-graph |

*A DWARF standing on the shoulders
of a GIANT
can sometimes see FARTHER
than the
GIANT HIMSELF!*

un- (means the reverse of)

un-zip	un-like	un-kind
un-able	un-seen	un-cov-er
un-done	un-hap-py	un-luck-y

dis- (means the reverse of)

dis-able	dis-a-gree	dis-col-or
dis-pose	dis-o-bey	dis-cov-er

inter- (means between two things)

inter-act	inter-com	inter-lock
inter-mix	inter-change	inter-view

super- (means extra, or above)

super-mom	super-heat
super-son-ic	super-vise
super-vi-sor	super-no-va
super-hu-man	super-pow-er
super-sen-si-tive	super-mar-ket
super-in-ten-dent	super-im-pose

The DIFFICULTIES in life are meant to make us BETTER, not BITTER!

re-dis-cov-er super-no-va
rediscover supernova

inter-view super-mom
interview supermom

un-hap-py super-vi-sor
unhappy supervisor

inter-view super-pow-er
interview superpower

sub-merge sub-ma-rine
submerge submarine

pre-judge super-in-ten-dent
prejudge superintendent

sub-arc-tic super-mar-ket
subarctic supermarket

super-sen-si-tive auto-mo-bile
supersensitive automobile

The best and most beautiful things in the world cannot be SEEN or TOUCHED,
but are FELT in the HEART!

You have been introduced to suffixes in previous lessons—here are some more. (The "-tion" or "-sion" suffix is pronounced "shun.")

shun=-tion   shun=-sion

sta-tion	ac-tion	vi-sion
na-tion	ad-di-tion	mis-sion
por-tion	ad-dic-tion	ex-ten-sion
sec-tion	at-ten-tion	ex-plo-sion
va-ca-tion	af-fec-tion	ex-pres-sion
pro-mo-tion	in-vi-ta-tion	im-pres-sion
ed-u-ca-tion	foun-da-tion	tel-e-vi-sion

-able

dur-able	en-able	dis-able
de-sir-able	ca-pable	no-table
a-dor-able	val-u-able	port-able
rea-son-able	pass-able	print-able
for-mi-dable	in-ca-pable	prob-able
pre-sent-able	per-ish-able	de-lec-table
pre-vent-able	im-prob-able	con-sid-er-able
in-es-cap-able	in-com-pa-rable	in-dis-pen-sable

> *When you were born, YOU cried and the WORLD rejoiced.*
> *Live your life in such a way that when you come to die,*
> *the WORLD cries, and YOU rejoice!*

-ness

good-ness	thick-ness	ill-ness
kind-ness	weak-ness	dark-ness
mad-ness	soft-ness	well-ness
nice-ness	bad-ness	wil-der-ness

-ful (means full of)

arm-ful	hope-ful	fear-ful
faith-ful	care-ful	pain-ful
play-ful	harm-ful	use-ful
won-der-ful	for-get-ful	thank-ful

-less (means without)

rest-less	reck-less	need-less
shift-less	help-less	end-less
worth-less	price-less	time-less
hope-less	point-less	home-less

-ment

place-ment	move-ment	treat-ment
state-ment	base-ment	a-bate-ment
pun-ish-ment	re-place-ment	re-fresh-ment
pave-ment	en-gage-ment	gov-ern-ment

WHO is right is never as important as WHAT is right!

won-der-ful in-vi-ta-tion
wonderful invitation

pre-sent-able gov-ern-ment
presentable government

in-com-pa-rable va-ca-tion
incomparable vacation

in-dis-pen-sable foun-da-tion
indispensable foundation

for-mi-dable mis-sion
formidable mission

de-sir-able pro-mo-tion
desirable promotion

a-dor-able ex-pres-sion
adorable expression

price-less wil-der-ness
priceless wilderness

The WORST PRISON of all is the one inside of a CLOSED HEART…

COMPOUND WORDS

A COMPOUND WORD is made by joining two complete words together to make a new word. It's fun to read the list below and determine which two words each one is made of! Compound words are *always* divided into the smaller words from which they are composed.

any-thing	hill-side	under-stand
classroom	without	bedroom
somebody	freeway	downtown
paycheck	clipboard	homework
sunrise	brainwash	earthquake
outdoors	supermarket	workout
datebook	overcome	pathways
superman	buckskin	footbridge
daybreak	hunchback	something
crackdown	tablecloth	underworld
playground	ballgame	homesick
	roommate	rosewood
	underground	footsteps

We can't stop the WAVES, but we can learn to SURF!

"BUILDING BLOCKS"

In each group of words, the top word is a part of every word listed below it. You will be *building words* from *blocks of syllables*. Try it…it's *fun!*

board
board-ing
key-board
clip-board

check
check-er
re-check
pay-check

rage
en-rage
en-rag-ing
out-ra-geous

pass
under-pass
sur-pass-ing
un-sur-pass-able

back
back-ing
back-ward
out-back

front
front-ward
con-front
con-fron-ta-tion

press
ex-press
in-ex-press-ible
com-press-ing

cover
un-cover
un-re-cover-able
dis-cover-ing

May we have the grace
to ACCEPT the things we cannot change…
the courage to CHANGE the things we can…
and the WISDOM to know the DIFFERENCE!

mark
re-mark
re-mark-able
un-re-mark-able

sense
non-sense
sens-i-tive
super-sens-i-tive

come
wel-come
wel-com-ing
over-com-ing

force
en-force
force-ful-ness
re-in-force-ment

see
fore-see
fore-see-able
un-fore-see-able

give
for-give
for-giv-able
un-for-giv-able

fort
com-fort
ef-fort
for-tress
ef-fort-less
com-fort-able
com-fort-ing-ly

agree
agree-able
agree-ment
agree-ing
dis-agree
dis-agree-able
dis-agree-ment

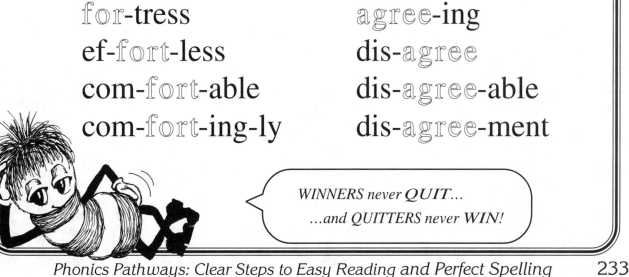

WINNERS never QUIT...
...and QUITTERS never WIN!

tend	**tract**
in-tend	sub-tract
in-tend-ing	sub-tract-able
super-in-ten-dent	un-sub-tract-able
under	**land**
under-stand	land-mark
mis-under-stand	play-land
mis-under-stand-ing	out-land-ish
mark	**pen**
mar-ket	play-pen
mar-ket-ing	pen-cil
mar-ket-able	in-dis-pen-sa-ble
mar-ket-a-bil-i-ty	car-pen-ter
sent	**press**
pre-sent	im-press
pre-sent-ed	im-pres-sion
pre-sent-able	im-pres-sion-able
un-pre-sent-able	im-pres-sion-is-tic

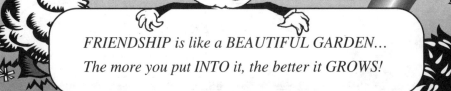

FRIENDSHIP is like a BEAUTIFUL GARDEN...
The more you put INTO it, the better it GROWS!

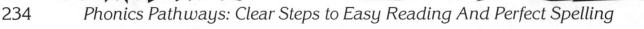

His won-der-ful, re-mark-able auto-mo-bile
has a super-sen-si-tive inter-com.

A super-no-va is a fan-tas-tic star that can
sud-den-ly shine a bil-lion times bright-er!

He seems to have a hope-less ad-dic-tion to
worth-less tel-e-vi-sion pro-grams.

She went to con-sid-er-able length to be help-ful
af-ter that dev-as-tat-ing earth-quake.

I have the im-pres-sion that Gus loves end-less
por-tions of de-lec-table re-fresh-ments.

It is im-prob-able that we will dis-cov-er any
more gold in that hill-side wil-der-ness.

Aus-tra-lia has out-land-ish-ly huge croc-o-diles
in its re-mark-able out-back.

Life itself can't give you joy,
    unless you really WILL it...
Life just gives you
        time and space...
It's up to YOU to FILL IT!

Supermom's performance went fantastically well.

It is time to submerge the submarine. *NOW!*

I'm cold! This must be a subarctic supermarket.

Gus thinks he is going on a formidable mission.

Her cats possess the most adorable expressions.

Soon she is going on an incomparable vacation.

Phonics is an unsurpassable tool for reading.

His expression at that moment was unprintable.

A strong foundation to a house is indispensable.

…And now, my re-gret-ful but un-a-void-able and in-es-cap-able con-clu-sion is that we have just fin-ished this in-ten-sive and sub-stan-tial book. This is the END! GOODBYE

We are all travelers as we pass over

the hills and valleys of life...

But the journey of a thousand miles

STILL begins with

JUST

ONE

STEP...

As did your journey through Phonics Pathways.

So where will you go now?

And what will you do?

It's a choice that's entirely up to YOU!

But wherever you go

and whatever you do...

"THIS ABOVE ALL...

TO THINE OWN SELF

BE TRUE!"

Thank you for letting my work
become part of your lives.

Dolores

–William Shakespeare

SPELLING STRATEGIES

Initially *Phonics Pathways* can be treated as just an "exposure" experience that will sensitize your students to the logic of the English language, and introduce them to the concept that specific rules do exist that determine exactly how words are spelled.

By the end of the book, however, it may be time to begin teaching spelling in earnest. Spelling and reading enhance one another in a synergistic fashion—accurate spelling promotes accurate reading, and vice versa. And it's certainly easier to remember one rule for many words than it is learning how to spell each word individually! (It's also very handy as well as economical to have reading and spelling programs available together in just one book.)

Have one notebook with three divided sections in it for each student—one section for copywork, one for dictation, and one for "trouble words." Copywork is always the best way to begin spelling lessons. Proceed as follows:

1 — Have students turn to the Copy section of their notebooks. Begin with the first spelling lesson in the book, the "c-k" rule on page 51. Explain the rule, and have students read some of the words again. Have them copy from five to ten words.

2 — Older students should copy the rule itself as a header on top of the page, but younger students probably will not be ready for this much writing activity just yet. Check work, have students correct errors.

3 — Have students turn to the Dictation section of their workbooks. Review the rule orally, and dictate about five to ten words for them to write down. Check work, and have students correct any errors by rewriting the word correctly three times.

4 — Students should keep a log of any spelling mistakes that were made in the "Trouble Words" section of their notebook. Always include these words in the next day's dictation and use them in a spelling test once a week as well.

5 — The next day see if *they* can tell *you* what the rule is. Offer whatever help is needed. Keep dictating words from that lesson until the student can write the words from dictation without error.

6 — After awhile begin dictating phrases and sentences, and not just the words. If dictation is limited to word families alone students may not be able to spell the word outside of context. Only when students spell words correctly in sentences can you be absolutely certain that the spelling rule has been truly and thoroughly integrated. This activity helps develop memory and concentration as well.

For variety try spelling with tile manipulatives, with magnetic letters, on individual whiteboards or on a chalkboard. Work only about 10-15 minutes at a time when writing. Little hands and fingers *do* get tired!

SPELLING & PRONUNCIATION CHART

SHORT VOWELS

ă	ĕ	ĭ	ŏ	ŭ
a cat	e pet	i hid	o top	u pup oo flood
al half	ea deaf	y gym	a want	o won a was
augh laugh	ai again	ui build		ou young

LONG-VOWELS

ā	ē	ī	ō
a-e tape ey they	e-e Pete ie field	i-e pine ie pie	o-e home oe toe
ai rain ea steak	e we i marine	i kind y try	o told ow row
ay say ei veil	ea meat y funny	uy buy igh right	oa soap ough dough
eigh eight	ee seed ei ceiling	ui guide	

LONG-VOWELS

ōo=ū	yōo=ū
u-e June ue blue	u-e pure
oo moon ui fruit	ew mew
o do ou soup	
ew new wo two	

SCHWA

ə=ŭ	
a sofa	o gallop
e spoken	u focus
i sanity	

MISCELLANEOUS

ô	ŏo
aw saw o dog	oo look
au haul al salt	u put
ough bought all tall	oul could
augh taught alk walk	

DIPHTHONGS

oi	ou
oi boil	ou out
oy toy	ow how

SPELLING & PRONUNCIATION CHART

CONSONANTS

k	f	j	z
k kid ke bake x tax c cat qu quiz ck sick ic picnic ch school ick picnicking	f fat ff huff gh rough ph phone	j just ge page dge fudge	z zip s is zz fizz se rose

CONSONANTS

sh	th	s	l	ch
sh ship s sure ti nation si mansion	th thin t̶h̶ this	s sat ss fuss c city ce race	l lap ll bell le noodle	ch chat tch hatch

CONSONANTS

wh	zh
wh- when	z azure s measure g beige

NG, NK ENDINGS

-ng	-nk
ing sing ang sang ong song ung sung	ink sink ank sank onk honk unk hunk

R-MODIFIED VOWELS

är	ôr	ʉr	âr
ar art	or for ore more ar warm our pour oor door oar roar	er her ir sir ur turn or work ear heard	are care air pair ear bear ere there eir their

Phonics Pathways: Clear Steps to Easy Reading and Perfect Spelling

PLURAL SPELLING CHART

-s   To make most words plural, just add "-s":

top	tops	duck	ducks	pet	pets
tent	tents	sock	socks	melt	melts
cake	cakes	pine	pines	bean	beans
date	dates	ride	rides	feed	feeds

-es   For words ending in "-sh," "-ch," "-tch," "-zz," "x," or "ss," add "-es":

fish	fishes	inch	inches	batch	batches
fizz	fizzes	miss	misses	tax	taxes
pinch	pinches	kiss	kisses	ditch	ditches
hiss	hisses	itch	itches	rich	riches

-ies   For words ending in "-y," change "-y" to "-i" and then add "-es":

ruby	rubies	penny	pennies	baby	babies
pansy	pansies	party	parties	hurry	hurries
try	tries	fly	flies	cry	cries
fry	fries	sky	skies	cry	cries

-ves   For words ending in "-f," change "-f" to "-v" and then add "-es":

loaf	loaves	wolf	wolves	leaf	leaves
elf	elves	life	lives	shelf	shelves
wife	wives	thief	thieves	leaf	leaves

SUFFIX SPELLING CHART

(See also page 111)

When adding a suffix beginning with a vowel: If a word ends in "y" preceded by a *consonant*, change "y" to "i" first. Exception: Keep the "y" when adding "ing":

-y

try	tries	tried	trying
study	studies	studied	studying
silly	sillier	silliest	
bumpy	bumpier	bumpiest	

When a word ends in "y" preceded by a *vowel*, most of the time just add the suffix:

-y

play	player	played	playing
employ	employer	employed	employing

When a word ends in "ie," drop the final "e" when adding a suffix beginning with a vowel. Exception: *Change* the "ie" to "y" when adding "ing":

-ie

lie	lies	lied	lying
tie	ties	tied	tying
die	dies	died	dying

Usually a word is not changed at all when adding a suffix beginning with a *consonant:*

dry	dryness	tie	tieless
use	useful	care	careful
bone	boneless	home	homeless

Phonics Pathways: Clear Steps to Easy Reading and Perfect Spelling   243

STUDENT ACHIEVEMENT CHART

NAME_____ AGE_____ GRADE_____

PHONE_____BEGAN TUTORING_____ENDED_____

SKILL LEVEL IN *PHONICS PATHWAYS*	REVIEW PAGE	DATE BEGUN	DATE COMPLETED
Short vowels through review	14		
Two-letter blends through review	36		
Three-letter short-vowel words through review	47		
C/k beginnings & -ck endings through review	55		
Double-consonant endings through review	67		
"-y" endings through review	71		
"-sh" and "-th" endings through review	77		
"-ch, -tch" endings through review	79		
"-ng" & "-nk" endings through review	86		
Long "a" words (silent "e" ending) through review	89		
Long "i" words (silent "e" ending) through review	91		
Long "o" words (silent "e" ending) through review	93		
Long "u" words (silent "e" ending) through review	95		
Long "e" words (silent "e" ending) through review	99		
All long vowel words through review	105		
Short-vowel suffixes through review	109		
Short and long-vowel suffixes through review	112		
Multisyllable words	114		
Consonant digraph beginnings through review	128		
Double-consonant beginnings through review	139		
"R" modified vowel words through review	154		
Long-vowel digraph words through review	168		
Vowel dipthong words through review	176		
"J" = "gi, gh, -dge" words through review	179		
"-y, -ie" and "-f = ves" words through review	182		
"oo = oo, ou, u" words through review	185		
"ô = au, aw, al, all, o" words through review	189		
Three-consonant beginning words through review	193		
Short-vowel spelling patterns through review	200		

Phonics Pathways: Clear Steps to Easy Reading and Perfect Spelling

STUDENT PROGRESS NOTES

NAME_____PHONE_____

DATE	PAGE	TUTOR NOTES	(Special help, extra review, recommendations, etc.)	TUTOR

VISION AND MOTOR COORDINATION TRAINING EXERCISES*

These exercises are designed to improve eye-hand-body coordination. Some experts feel they will also develop eye tracking ability. Not all children will be able to do all of these exercises. Try working through them, and see if you can come up with a small group of them that you both enjoy. It is important to practice the ones you have chosen on a regular basis, but you can vary them if you feel a change is needed:

1. Have him hold his head still, and follow with his eyes as you slowly move a small object (penny, head of pencil, etc.) from far left to far right at eye level, back and forth several times. Now move it up and down, and diagonally. Then slowly bring the pencil in towards his nose while he focuses as long as he can, and out as far as you can reach. Always move very slowly and smoothly.

2. Make a beanbag about 5 inches square (birdseed makes *wonderful* filling!) and throw it back and forth to him. (Beanbags are easy to catch and don't roll away when dropped.) Aim for a faster throw and catch. (He may wish to change to a ball when this skill is well developed.)

3. Have him lie on the ground, and tell him to raise his left leg, right leg, left arm, or right arm. After he can raise the correct leg or arm easily, have him try a combination of two together: "Left leg, right arm," etc.

4. While he is on the ground, tell him to make "angels in the snow": to move his arms and legs up and down against the ground. Then name a particular arm or leg, as in the above exercise. When he gets proficient, have him combine an arm with a leg upon command, as above.

5. Have him walk on a balance board (holding his hands if necessary), or some variation of it. If this is too difficult, have him walk all along a rope that has been laid across the floor, one foot in front of the other.

6. Have him march to an even beat throwing opposite arms and legs forward, while you clap or beat a drum. Then have him clap and march at the same time.

7. See if he can crawl. If he cannot, have him practice crawling.

8. If a trampoline is available, have him jump on a trampoline. Hold his hand for safety!

9. If he is well coordinated, have him practice skipping.

*No special claims for these exercises are made, other than that they were helpful to the author's own children. They may or may not be helpful to others. Check with your doctor before proceeding.

10. Suspend a whiffle ball (plastic ball with cutouts) from the ceiling or rafter in the garage, about chest level. Have him "box" with alternate fists, aiming for a smooth, even stroke. Then have him hit the ball with a paddle or a bat, always trying to move it in the same center direction.

11 Suspend a whiffle ball at foot level, slightly off the floor. Have him kick with alternate feet, aiming for a smooth, even kick, sending the ball in the same center direction each time. After a while, as he kicks with his left foot have him move his right arm slightly forward, and his left arm slightly back, alternating arms with legs.

THE FOLLOWING EXERCISES HELP DEVELOP MANUAL DEXTERITY:

12. Have him make large circles with both hands at the same time (chalk on blackboard or fingers on wall). Then reverse direction. Now have him cross his hands over and *repeat* this exercise, if he can. This may be too difficult for many children, but is very useful if it can be managed.

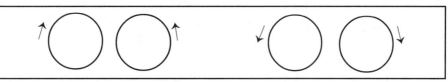

13. Have him crumple up a sheet of paper into a small ball, using only one hand. Then repeat with the other hand. (Tissue paper is easiest; also try newspaper and writing paper.)

14. Sandpaper *greatly* increases the tactile experience! Cut out large, 3 to 6 inch letters from sandpaper, and glue them onto cardboard. Have him feel each letter with his fingers as he names the letter sound. Then have him trace it with his fingertip, and say the sound again.

15. To increase the kinesthetic experience, tell him to trace *big* letters with his fingertip on the wall (or chalk on blackboard if available).

16. Tracing is *great!* Get tracing paper, and have him trace some of his favorite pictures with a pencil. Later on have him trace large letters, and then progressively smaller ones. Always make sure he begins at the correct point and moves his pencil in the right direction.

17. Have him draw the following, using one continuous motion when possible:

PYRAMID (See also page 50)

Practice these words until you are able to read them smoothly—each block of words has the same short-vowel sound. This part of *Pyramid* will help you blend letters into words (as will the exercises on page 38). (If you *do* find this kind of reading practice helpful, there is a whole book of pyramids available from Dorbooks.)

Next, read the *Pyramid* on the opposite page, which is comprised of the same words. This part of *Pyramid* will help you build words into sentences. Your eye-tracking will *strengthen* and your eye span *lengthen!*

> *The road UPHILL and the road DOWNHILL*
> *are the SAME ONE!*

a	c-a	ca	ca-t	cat	
a	f-a	fa	fa-t	fat	
a	h-a	ha	ha-d	had	
a	b-a	ba	ba-g	bag	
a	a-n	an	an-d	and	
i	i-n	in			
i	h-i	hi	hi-d	hid	
i	b-i	bi	bi-g	big	
i	f-i	fi	fi-g	fig	figs
o	B-o	Bo	Bo-b	Bob	
u	g-u	gu	gu-m	gum	
u	n-u	nu	nu-t	nut	nuts

It's a *REAL CHALLENGE*
to climb the ladder of success...
For you must keep your:
    EYES on the ball,
    EARS to the ground,
    NOSE to the grindstone,
    HANDS on the wheel, and
    FEET on the path...
But the view from the top is
    FANTASTIC!

PEAK OF SUCCESS →

Bob

Bob had

Bob had a bag.

Bob had a big bag.

Bob hid gum in his big bag.

Bob hid gum and figs in his big bag.

Bob hid gum, figs, and nuts in his big bag.

Bob hid gum, figs, nuts, and a fat cat in his bag.

Bob hid gum, figs, nuts, and a big fat cat in his bag.

✹ HOT TIPS

1. *Echo:* (For short-vowel sounds) Make a list of about 10 words that *begin* with the short-vowel sound you are working on, such as the ă in "apple," using the picture words from the short ă page. Sprinkle in about 5 words that do not begin with that sound, such as "rug," etc.

   Mix the words up, and read them slowly with emphasis. Students should repeat the word if you say a word beginning with that sound, but put their hand over their mouth and say nothing if the word begins with *another* sound. Repeat this activity with the rest of the vowels as they are learned.

2. *All In A Row:* (For short-vowel words) Have five students stand in a row in front of the class, each one holding up a sheet of paper with a very large vowel written on it. Read words containing random short-vowel sounds, each time choosing a student to go up and stand by the person holding the correct vowel and say the vowel sound. (For individuals, tack posters of each sound to the wall and have your learner walk to the correct poster, stand by it, and say the sound. Also see #3 and #4 on page 3.)

3. *You're On The Air:* Everyone opens their book and reads the same page. Walk around with a portable microphone, and choose a student randomly to read out loud into the microphone. All students should follow along, reading silently and running their finger under the word/sentence being read. Each one must be ready to be "on the air," as nobody knows who'll be chosen next!

4. *Fishing Marathon:* Copy the page you are working on and cut the words into equal sizes. Fold each word in two and put them in an empty tissue box. Divide the class into two groups. Students take turns reaching in the box, catching a "fish" and reading it. The first group to finish wins the fishing marathon!

5. *Life Boat:* Put 8 "lifeboats" (carpet-squares, towels, etc.) on the floor in a row. Eight students march around them while you read a variety of words, most of which contain the sound you are working on but some of which do not. When you read a word *not* having that sound they must sit on or touch a lifeboat. Remove one lifeboat each time. Students must share the dwindling supply until only one lifeboat is left. (Make sure it is the biggest one!)

6. *Musical Chairs:* Put 9 chairs in a row, every other one facing backwards. Eight students circle the chairs while you read a variety of words, most of which contain the sound you are working on but some of which do not. When you read a word *not* having that sound the students scramble to sit down. The student left standing goes back to his seat. Remove a chair and keep playing until only one student is left.

7. *Treasure Hunt:* Copy the page you are working on, cut the words, phrases, or sentences into equal sizes, and fold them up. Hide them around the room, and see who can find the most "treasures!" They must read each note as it is found. (Consider having a little treat folded up in some of them to make the game more enticing!)

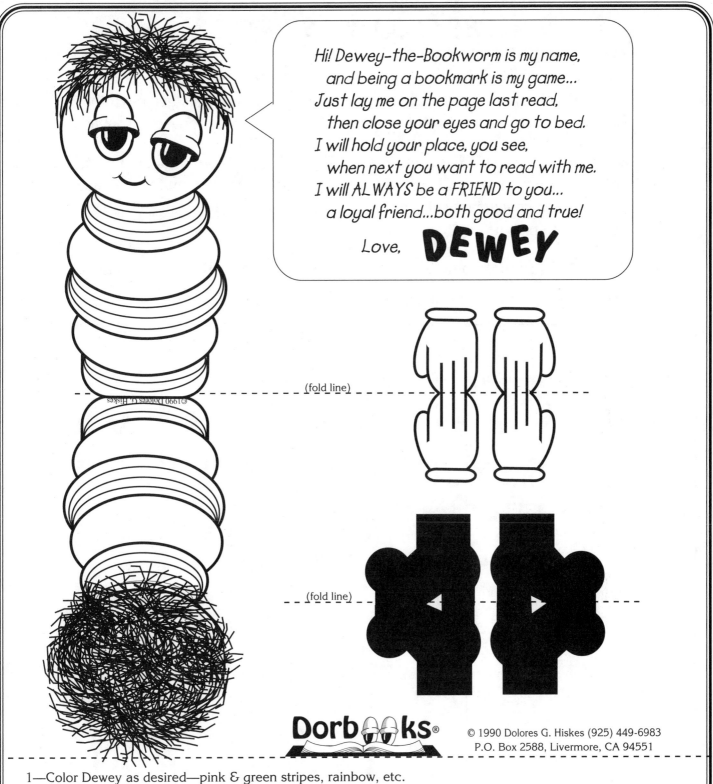

Hi! Dewey-the-Bookworm is my name,
and being a bookmark is my game...
Just lay me on the page last read,
then close your eyes and go to bed.
I will hold your place, you see,
when next you want to read with me.
I will ALWAYS be a FRIEND to you...
a loyal friend...both good and true!

Love, **DEWEY**

(fold line)

(fold line)

© 1990 Dolores G. Hiskes

Dorbooks®

© 1990 Dolores G. Hiskes (925) 449-6983
P.O. Box 2588, Livermore, CA 94551

1—Color Dewey as desired—pink & green stripes, rainbow, etc.
2—Cut out Dewey's body, gloves, and shoes.
3—Cut two pieces of 5 or 6 inch-long black yarn for his arms and legs.
4—Wipe glue thickly all over the *wrong* side of Dewey's body.
5—Place two yarn strips on his body as illustrated, over the wet glue.
6—Fold Dewey in half, glue sides together, and press until firm.
7—Glue wrong sides of hands & feet, fold in half over yarn ends, press until firm.
8—Cover Dewey with a heavy book overnight, or until thoroughly dry.
9—Trim Dewey with scissors to even front and back edges, if necessary.

(Want *sparkly eyes*? Slit across lower eyelids, glue backs of two large black sequins, and insert halfway under lids!)

251

THE SHOO-FLY SHUFFLE

This is really another version of *The Short-Vowel Shuffle* (see page 4 for complete directions) but we can't call it that anymore because this game will be used with syllables and words from this point on, and not short-vowel sounds.

Why don't we call it *"The Shoo-fly Shuffle?"* In fact, *Shoo-fly* actually was a Civil War nonsense song once. Originally it was kind of a shuffling dance, so that's a good name for it because shuffling around your desk is one very good way to play it!

("Shoo-fly" can mean other things as well, such as a pie filled with molasses and brown sugar. *(Mmmmmmmm…)*

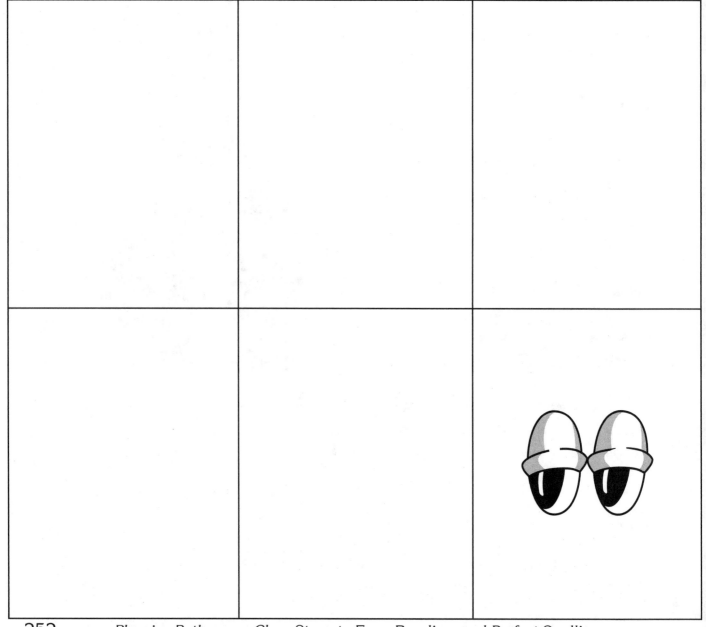

See page 18 for complete instructions. This game can be very helpful in easing the blending transition all the way from three-letter words to multisyllable words:

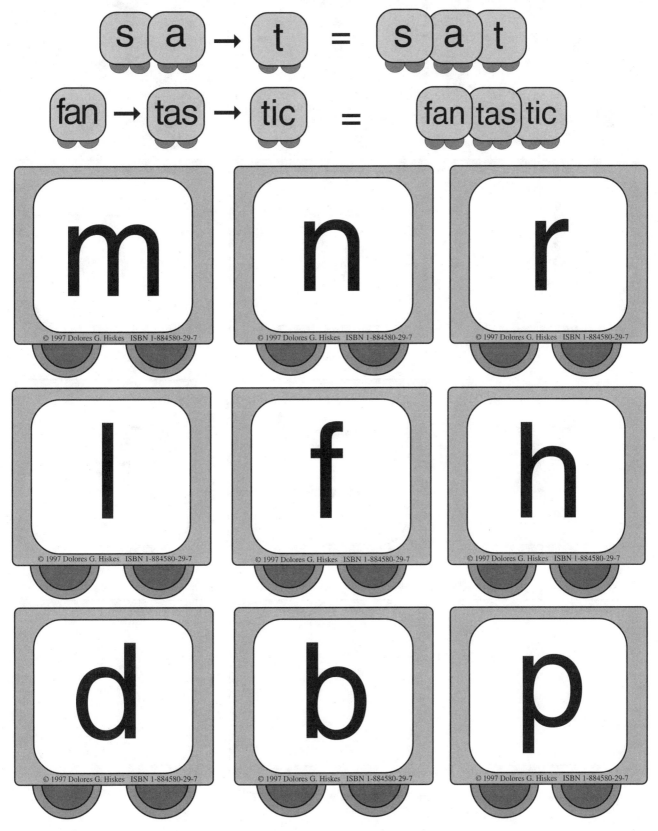

Phonics Pathways: Clear Steps to Easy Reading and Perfect Spelling   253

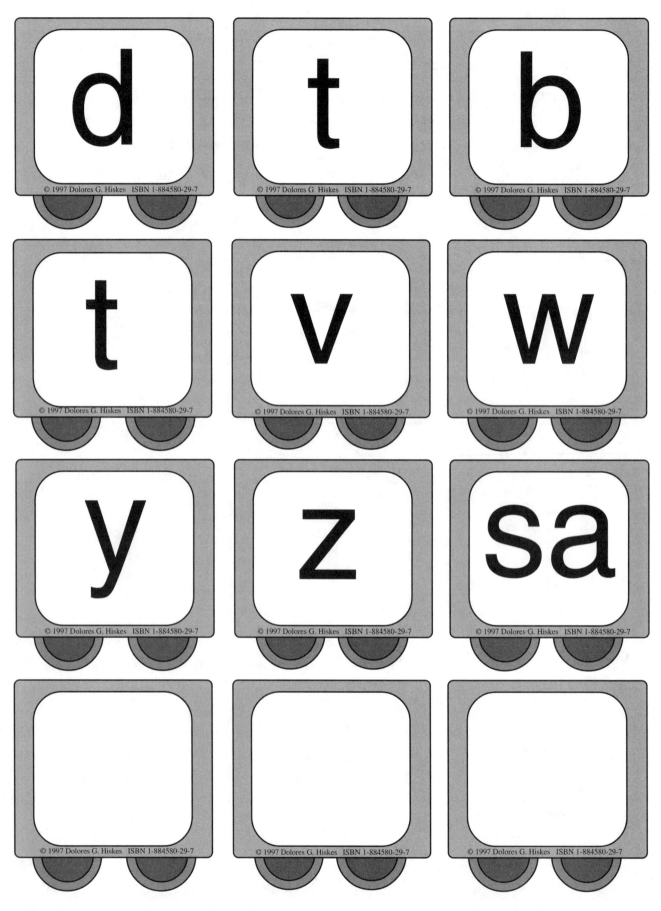

Phonics Pathways: Clear Steps to Easy Reading and Perfect Spelling

BLENDIT! (Similar to *Bingo*)

See page 14 for complete directions. *Blendit!* can be played with two, three, or four players. Good readers can be paired with less able students because everyone has an equal chance of winning. Everyone loves to play a *Bingo*-type game, and it's certainly a great way to reinforce learning!

Phonics Pathways: Clear Steps to Easy Reading And Perfect Spelling   255

$\mathcal{S}$TARSEARCH

See page 35 for complete directions and a sample game on page 36. It's always lots of fun to go "stargazing!" (Here's another challenge: see if you can count the *number* of stars you have gathered. Can you count that high yet?)

Phonics Pathways: Clear Steps to Easy Reading and Perfect Spelling

BAG THE BUGS

Complete instructions are on page 46, and a sample game is shown on page 47. It can be played by a single player, or with small-to-medium groups if you make up sufficient cards. (This game is always a favorite—students *love* those bugs!)

Phonics Pathways: Clear Steps to Easy Reading and Perfect Spelling

Appendix C—A Word About Curriculum and State Standards

Phonics Pathways is grounded in scientifically based reading research, as analyzed by the National Reading Panel, published in 2000, and required by schools receiving Reading First funds. As determined by the National Reading Panel, children who learn to read through a systematic, sequential, and explicit phonics-based approach make more progress than children who learn to read without such instruction. *Phonics Pathways* provides clear steps for systematic and explicit phonetic instruction. Students quickly become decoders; they learn to readily recognize words and, with practice, become fluent readers.

The National Reading Panel emphasizes the need for instruction in the five essential reading components: phonemic awareness, phonics, fluency, vocabulary, and comprehension. *Phonics Pathways* provides a way for *all* learners to acquire the fundamentals of phonemic awareness while gaining a strong ability to decode.

Lessons begin with single short-vowel sounds, move to two-letter blends, progress to simple three-letter words such as "cat" and "hen," and gradually advance to challenging words of several syllables such as "formidable" or "outrageous." Through multiple and repeated readings of words, phrases, sentences, and short passages, students quickly become fluent readers. *Phonics Pathways* provides the added bonus of spelling instruction that is tied to the phonics lessons, maximizing the effect of the lesson and making excellent use of instructional time.

Phonics Pathways is in alignment with academic content standards across the nation. The format of these standards varies from state to state but the content is similar. For example, the following California Reading Standards for third grade are supported by instruction found on pages 113–114 and 225–229 in *Phonics Pathways*:

> 1.2 Decode regular multisyllabic words.
> 1.8 Use knowledge of prefixes (e.g., un-, re-, pre-, bi-, mis-, dis-)
> and suffixes (e.g., -er, -est, -ful) to determine the meaning of words.

Relative academic content standards for reading may be found on the next pages, spanning several grade levels and distilled from a number of different states. In most cases these standards are related to language arts skills and competencies in California, Florida, New York, North Carolina, Ohio, Illinois, and Texas. Each state has its own guidelines for suggested curriculum from which a school district can determine its course of study.

Standards are ultimately determined at the state level, with input from people all over the state and from local communities as well. Some areas have a State Board of Education, appointed to oversee the selection and the writing of standards. Committees with representatives from teacher groups, colleges, universities, learned societies, parents, and even student groups have served on many of the committees.

Teachers should consider the following information as suggestions for standards compliance. Ultimately, a teacher's professional judgment is key to making an appropriate standards alignment based upon their own state's guidelines.

Standards: Phonemic Awareness

Learner can hear, identify, and manipulate letter sounds (phonemes) individually and in spoken words. Learner can identify and produce rhyming words in response to an oral prompt, and distinguish orally stated one-syllable words and separate into beginning or ending sounds. Phonemic awareness is the understanding that the sounds of spoken language work together to make words.

Phonics Pathways Alignment: Phonemic Awareness

Research indicates that many young children cannot extract an individual sound from hearing it within a word (*Becoming A Nation of Readers*, The Report of the Commission on Reading, The National Instisute of Education, U.S. Department of Education, 1985).

Every letter introduced is illustrated with multiple pictures *beginning* with that sound. Students name each picture and then isolate and say the beginning sound, associating that sound with the vowel being learned. After that, students listen for this sound within a word using games and activities and think of other words beginning with that sound. Multiple pictures provide the subtle variation and range comprising each letter sound.

Individual short-vowel sounds (pages 3–14)
Consonants and blends (pages 15–36)
Reinforcement is provided by repeated practice and with auditory discrimination games:

    Short-Vowel Stick (page 3) short-vowel reference
    Short-Vowel Shuffle (page 4) teaches short-vowel sounds
    Blendit! (pages 14, 255) reinforces short-vowel sounds
    Lifeboat (page 250) listens for and discriminates short-vowel sound within the word
    Echo (page 250) listens for and discriminates short-vowel sound within the word
    Musical Chairs (page 250) listens for and discriminates sound within the word

Standards: Blending

Learner will be able to read letters and track from left to right, moving sequentially from sound to sound by blending letters orally into syllables. Learner will spell blends from dictation, and can identify and produce rhyming words in response to an oral prompt, and understand sameness/difference when one sound is substituted for another. Learner will be able to match all consonant and short-vowel sounds to appropriate letters.

Phonics Pathways Alignment: Two-Letter Syllables

Research indicates that teachers who spend more than average time on blending produce larger than average gains on first- and second-grade reading achievement tests. (*Becoming A Nation of Readers*, The Report of the Commission on Reading, The National Institute of Education, U.S. Department of Education, 1985).

Phonics Pathways has seventeen pages of two-letter blends to establish strong eye-tracking skills. Every consonant introduced is illustrated with multiple pictures beginning with that letter. Students orally name each picture and say the beginning sound, associating the consonant with that sound. Then students orally read the two-letter blends, first saying the letters separately and then blending them together into one smooth sound. Now students think of and say other words that begin with this blend, such as "su as in sum, supper," etc. Students begin to see the connevtion between letters, words, and meaning; and reading from left to right.

Consonants and two-letter blends (pages 15–36)
Reinforcement is provided by repeated practice and with special games:

    Train Game (pages 18, 253–254) a manipulative developing blending skills
    StarSearch (pages 35–36, 256) reinforces blending fluency

Standards: Simple Short-Vowel Words

Learner will be able to track auditorily each letter in a word and every word in a sentence, and understand that as letters of words change so do the sounds. Learner will be able to decode nonsense words and read text accurately. Learner can distinguish initial, medial, and final sounds in single-syllable short vowel words, and be able to spell them from dictation. Learner will be able to add, delete, or change target sounds to change words (e.g. pan, an).

Phonics Pathways Alignment: Simple Short-Vowel Words

Three-Letter Words (pages 37–73)
Pyramid (page 50, 248-249) Develops fluency by predictable text of gradually increasing length (beginning with a single word, moving to very long sentences)
K = C, K,-CK (pages 51-55)
Two-Consonant Endings (pages 56-67)
Twin-Consonant Endings (page 72)
Consonant Digraph Endings (pages 74-79)
Fluency Reality Check (Real and Nonsense Words)
Reinforcement is provided by repeated practice and with a wide variety of special games and activities:

> *Bag The Bugs* (pages 46–47, 257)
> *All In A Row* (page 250)
> *You're On The Air* (page 250)
> *Fishing Marathon* (page 250)
> *Treasure Hunt* (page 250)
> *Shoo-Fly Shuffle* (page 252)
> *The Train Game* (page 253)
> *Blendit!* (page 255)
> *StarSearch* (page 256)

(Note: Any of the above games and activities can be played with any lesson in *Phonics Pathways* from this point on.)

Standards: Complex Short-Vowel Spelling Patterns

Learner will be able to identify and read words with complex short vowel representation in isolation, text, and from dictation including dictated sentences. Learner will be able to read text accurately and fluently, select phonetic letter patterns, and blend those sounds into recognizable words. They will know how to translate them into oral and silent reading.

Phonics Pathways Alignment: Short-Vowel Spelling Patterns

Special Short-Vowel Spellings
OO=moon, oo=took, O=aw, au, al, all, o (pages 183–189)
E=ea, ai ; I=y, ui; O=a, U=o, ou, oo, a, schwa (pages 194–200)

Diphthongs
Oi, oy, ou, ow (pages 169–176)

Standards: Long-Vowel Spelling Patterns

Learner will be able to identify and read words with long vowel representation in isolation, text, and from dictation, and be able to read text accurately and fluently, distinguishing between long- and short-vowel sounds in words. Learner will know and use complex word families when reading (e.g., -igh) to decode unfamiliar words. Learner will be able to spell and apply various phonetic patterns for words with long-vowel sounds, including dictated sentences.

Phonics Pathways **Alignment: Long-Vowel Spelling Patterns**

Simple long-vowel sounds (pages 87–105)
Special long- and short-vowel discrimination exercise (pages 103-104)
E=ei (page 170)
Long-vowel digraphs (pages 155---168)
      ai, ay, ie, oa, oe, ow, oo, ew, ue, ui, ou
I=igh (page 208)
O=ough (page 209)
Long-A spelling patterns (pages 211–213)
      ei, eigh, ey, ea

Standards: R-Controlled Words

Learner will be able to identify, read, and spell words with r-controlled vowels in isolation and in text, including dictated sentences.

Phonics Pathways **Alignment: R-Controlled Words**

-ar.- or, -oor, -ore, -our, -oar, -er,- ir, -ur, -ear (pages 145–154)
-are, -air, -er, -ere (pages 219–220)

Standards: Initial Consonant Blends

Learner will be able to identify, read, and spell words beginning with two or three consonant blends in isolation and in text, including dictated sentences.

Phonics Pathways **Alignment: Initial Consonant Blends**

Two-consonant beginnings (pages 129-144)
      bl-, fl-, pl-, cl-, gl-, sl-, sm-, sn-,st-, sp-, sc-, sk
Three-consonant beginnings (pages 190–193)
      str-, spl-, thr-, scr-, spr-

Standards: Plurals and Contractions

Learner will be able to identify, read, and spell regular and irregular plurals and possessives in isolation and in text, including dictated sentences. Learner will understand the mechanics of contractions and be able to accurately contract two words.

Phonics Pathways **Alignment: Plurals and Contractions**

-ng, -nk endings (pages 82–85)
Plural, possessive, and X (pages 116–117)
F=-ves (page 181)
Contractions (page 201)
Plural spelling chart (page 242)

Standards: Homophones, Homonyms, Homographs

Learner will be able to identify simple multiple-meaning words and use them correctly in text, and use knowledge of homonyms, homophones, and homographs to determine the meanings of words.

Phonics Pathways **Alignment: Homophones, Homonyms, Homographs**

Homophones, homonyms, homographs (pages 221–222)

Standards: Prefixes and Suffixes

Learner will be able to recognize changes in root/base word meanings when prefixes and suffixes are added as well as read and spell phonetic patterns for these words, including dictated sentences.

Phonics Pathways Alignment: Prefixes and Suffixes

-y suffix (page 68)
-ng, -nk endings (pages 82-85)
Short and long vowel single-syllable words with suffixes (pages 106–112)
Suffix spelling chart (page 111)
Adding -ic or -ick suffix to multisyllable words (page 114)
-Y, -ie plus suffixes (page 180)
Prefixes (pages 225–227)
       pre-, sub-, re-, auto-, un-, dis-, inter-, super-
Suffixes (pages 228–230)
       -tion, -sion, -able, -ness, -ful, -less, -ment
Suffix spelling chart (page 243)

Standards: Multisyllable Words

Learner will be able to decode regular multisyllabic words and compound words, and know how to syllabicate a word accurately. Learner will be able to read and spell multi syllable words in isolation or in dictated sentences, and use knowledge of individual words in unknown compound words to predict their meaning. Learner will be able to track auditorily each word in a sentence and every syllable in a word.

Phonics Pathways Alignment: Multisyllable Words

Multisyllable words (page 113)
Syllabication rules (page 115)
Multisyllable words with suffixes (page 223)
-ce, -ge, -able, -ible (page 224)
Prefixes and suffixes (pages 225–230)
Compound words (page 231)
Building blocks (pages 232–236)

Standards: Spelling

Learner will be able to spell independently by using knowledge of letter names, spelling rules, and of complex word families.

Phonics Pathways Alignment: Spelling

Research reveals that accurate spelling is critical to the reading process, and that skillful readers have internalized precise and detailed spellings of words and in a fraction of a second map them to the speech patterns they represent. Moreover, to the extent that this knowledge is underdeveloped or inaccurate, it is strongly associated with specific reading disability. (Adams, *Annals of Dyslexia* (Vol. 47, 1997).

Education Research Analysts, who evaluate textbooks for Texas state adoption, listed *Phonics Pathways* as their top-ranked program for spelling rules. They found 130 spelling rules, 36 more than the next highest-scoring reading programs.

In *Phonics Pathways* reading and spelling are taught as an integrated unit—each skill reinforces and enhances the other. Spelling rules are taught when the letter or sound is introduced, ranging from simple to complex. Additionally, it offers the following resources:

Spelling strategies (a simple step-by-step blueprint for teaching spelling—page 238)
Index to spelling rules and patterns (page 239)
Spelling and pronunciation chart (pages 240–241)
Plural spelling chart (page 242)
Suffix spelling chart (page 243)

Standards: Fluency

Fluency is the ability to read text accurately and quickly. It provides a bridge between word recognition and comprehension. Fluent readers recognize words and comprehend at the same time. Learner will practice, extend, and refine knowledge of letter-sound relationships by controlled and decodable practice reading.

Phonics Pathways Alignment:

Research indicates that in order to read skillfully children need practice in seeing and understanding decodable words in connected text (Adams, *Beginning to Read: Thinking and Learning about Print* (Center for the Study of Reading, The Reading Research and Education Center, University of Illinois, 1990). Research also shows that even students with the most serious reading problems can learn how to read if provided with effective code-based reading instruction (Shaywitz, etc. *Biological Psychiatry*), as reported in the New York Times, July 2003.

Fluency is promoted, developed, and integrated throughout *Phonics Pathways* with lavish examples and 100 percent decodable practice readings in every lesson. Extensive word lists, two-word phrases, and practice sentences using decodable text comprise every lesson, developing the speed, automaticity, and accuracy that is a necessary and integral part of fluency and comprehension in reading.

At times instructional methods have been tailored to students' perceptual styles or dominant modalities. These views are not supported by research. Eight separate reviews have all concluded that matching beginning reading methods to different aptitudes has not been proven effective. (Adams, *Beginning to Read: Thinking and Learning about Print,* Center for the Study of Reading, The Reading Research and Education Center, University of Illinois, 1990).

Phonics Pathways uses a multisensory method of teaching, addressing all learning styles. All children learn whether visual, auditory, or kinesthetic. A multisensory method of teaching has the synergistic effect of addressing the strongest modality while reinforcing the weakest.

Lowell School District in Whittier, CA implemented *Phonics Pathways* with all of their Title I students. At midyear comprehension scores for third grade went up an average of 26 National Percentile points, fourth grade 17 National Percentile points, fifth grade 8 National Percentile points, and sixth grade 22 National Percentile points. Bettina Dunne, reading teacher, concluded:

> "Phonics Pathways *is an invaluable aid to teaching phonics. It requires little or no preparation time and is appropriate for all grade levels.* Phonics Pathways *does not teach comprehension, but it unlocks the secrets of sound and symbol relationships allowing comprehension to become the focus. Students, now able to read words, can meet reading at its most vital level—they can read for meaning."*

CLASSROOM (Including ESL)

"Our school serves a diverse socio-economic population, with many students in the free and reduced lunch program, living in subsidized housing, and coming to school totally unprepared to learn. We established an in-school tutoring program with *Phonics Pathways,* using parent and community volunteers. First to third-grade nonreaders were tutored fifteen minutes a day, three days a week.

"In less than a year test results showed the school advanced from having the lowest to the highest reading scores in the entire school district. Our teachers are elated! Fourth-grade teacher Pam Mendonca now has all of these 'graduates' in her class for the first time, and she observed: *'This is the most literate class I have ever had. Our tutorial program is worth its weight in gold!'"*

—Joe Madeiros, Principal
Joe Michell School, Livermore, CA

"After only four months of using *Phonics Pathways* 100% of my bilingual Title One first-graders are reading the regular first-grade books. All of them have some level of limited English-speakihg ability and come from poor economic standings. One-third of my students have one or more parents serving time in prisons. They now have the strategies they need to read. The best part is the match to Spanish phonics—it follows the same sound patterns. Now my parent helpers are using it at home, and my colleagues are all using it as well. I've had great success creating a balanced reading program for my students using your materials along with our district program. Thank you for creating such an effective program for everyone—teachers, parents, and most of all for *students!"*

—Tracy Ciambrone, M.A.
Bilingual First Grade Teacher
San Jacinto, CA

"I have used *Phonics Pathways* as an excellent source of systematic phonics materials and ideas. It is yards ahead of available phonic workbooks and much more fun and interesting. It does not insult the student with "give-away pages" that lead to quick answers with little understanding or learning. The introduction, reading manual description, and hints are excellent. I especially liked the reading sentences, which take so long to make up on your own. Kids desperately want to be able to read, and phonics taught in such an interesting, systematic way gives them some success right away. Excitement soon replaces their fear and discouragement, and they're off to the races!"

—Diane Ransford, Teacher and Tutor
Orinda, CA

"As a classroom teacher, I have found a real need in our reading curricula for good, consistent phonics. Children need a solid, sequential program which builds upon previously learned skills with small, incremental steps toward the whole. Your program offers just the right degree in advances to ensure success. I have found that frustration is almost entirely eliminated with your books. *Phonics Pathways* provides a solid base from which to teach the basic sounds that make up our language. From a teacher's perspective, the little proverbs scattered throughout the book offer great insight and encouragement. I have found my students understand and appreciate them much more than expected."

—Susan Ebbers, Second-Grade Teacher
Livermore, CA

"Cristal, a Spanish girl in my second-grade class, could not read. Then I discovered your wonderful book. After three weeks she is progressing nicely with its orderly, step-by-step approach, and is delighted by the encouraging sayings and quotes. Her face just beams when I tell her *she* is the one climbing the oak tree to the top. Cristal is a different child! Thanks for turning the lights on for so many."

—Diane Sambrink, Teacher
Raleigh, NC

"The administration of Cesar E. Chavez Middle School and I thank you for *Phonics Pathways.* I have been using your phonics program for the past one and one-half years in my Learning Handicapped Special Day Class, with gratifying results. The students are delighted! Allow me to wish you continued success with your publishing endeavors."

—John Milton, Teacher
Hayward, CA

"*Phonics Pathways* takes all the guesswork and example-finding out of teaching reading. Each lesson is clearly laid out and accompanied by abundant examples that reinforce the point to be learned. Best of all, it is a complete program which meets the needs of *all* reading levels, from beginning to remedial. I use this book to complement and supplement the current school programs, which are so rich in literature. I really feel that I have finally found a winning combination that will provide students with the skill they need most of all in order to succeed—the skill of literacy. *Phonics Pathways* truly is a one-stop shopping dream!"

—Chris Cova,
Teacher and Tutor
Folsom, CA

HOME-SCHOOL

"I'm a new homeschooling Mom and was having tremendous success teaching my 8th grader with *Phonics Pathways*, but not until this month did I realize just how *much* success. He has been wearing glasses since 3rd grade—he had a muscle problem with astigmatism. We started with the book eight months ago, ten minutes a day. He had an eye exam last week, and now has 20/20 vision and is free from glasses—thanks to your eyerobics"! I cannot thank you enough for your incredible book."

—Wendi Cody Hill
Morgan Hill, CA

"This is an intensive and incremental approach to teaching reading. It can be used with any age, beginning or remedial. Older students would not find this manual insulting or babyish. I especially liked the large, easy-to-read typeface, and each page is visually interesting and uncluttered. If you want a no-frills approach to phonics that almost teaches itself, this book is certainly worth considering."

—Mary Pride, *Practical Homeschooling*

"*Phonics Pathways* is a complete program. Teaching instruction on each page is brief enough so that no preparation time is needed. Each new concept taught is followed by words, phrases and sentences for practice, so no other reading material is necessary. Because of quick movement into blending practice, children are reading three-letter words very soon. Reading practice is designed to improve left-to-right tracking skills, especially important for preventing dyslexic problems. *Phonics Pathways* is very reasonably priced for such a complete program."

—Cathy Duffy, Author
Christian Home Educators Curriculum Manual

"I have been using *Phonics Pathways* for approximately two years to teach my twins (now seven) how to read. I can't say enough good things about the program, and want to thank you profusely for developing it. This program has made such a difference in our family that I have continually recommended it. I used to work tutoring learning-disabled at a local community college, and they have ordered it on my recommendation."

—Kathleen Smith
Chico, CA

"We are home-schooling, and our nine- and seven-year-olds were convinced they would never read. We had spent well over $600 buying products to help our children learn, but would have been better off never to have bought a single one. Then I discovered *Phonics Pathways* in our local library. Now, only six months later, our oldest child reads anything he wants, and his sister is not far behind. We are absolutely thrilled with their progress and your book!"

—The Walter R. Wright family
Gnadenhutten, OH

"I never thought I would have to teach my children how to read at home. But by Christmas, my first-grader was coming home in tears saying that he was stupid since he couldn't read. Then I found your book. I knew exactly what to do and how to do it at each point, because each page has such clear directions. Your technique of putting new reading words in front of a sentence is just great. We spent only ten minutes a day working and ten months after we started he was a strong and successful reader with excellent comprehension. Best of all, his younger five-year-old brother learned along with him, and is now able to read simple books all by himself. *Phonics Pathways* has been a great success with my children. Please accept a heart-felt thank you!"

—Tasia Florey
Livermore, CA

"Using your book is one of the most exciting and gratifying experiences I've had as a parent. I'm so amazed at what our three-and-a-half year old is learning. She really enjoys Dewey the Bookworm, who makes each lesson such fun. Your program has empowered me to be able to do something I've always wanted to do but never knew how. I'm just thrilled with this program!"

—Julie Daly

"We are home-schooling and used what we thought to be 'good' phonics programs with our children, but all we achieved was frustration. Our older children did not begin reading until age nine. I had made a wish-list along the way of what I would like to see in a good phonics program. Naturally, it would be *user-friendly*—even for the Mom who had never taught phonics before. It would have a *minimum of sight words* which would be slowly introduced. Of course it would be *complete*, with separate readers not required. Most of all, *encouragement* for the teacher and student would continue throughout the lessons.

"*Phonics Pathways* is all of the above—plus more! Your explanation of dyslexia is simple and to the point. Our daughter has gone weekly to a Developmental Ophthalmologist, and the vision and motor coordination training exercises you have included in your book are the same exercises that she has done at home and in therapy. She is now improving by leaps and bounds. Thank you for offering to parents a very insightful phonics program."

——Jill Denly Creative Home Teaching
San Diego, CA

Phonics Pathways: Clear Steps to Easy Reading and Perfect Spelling

TUTORING (Remedial, Special Ed, ESL, Adult)

"In the heart of Silicon Valley live a number of students from non-English speaking families of all cultures who cannot read. A state-of-the-art YES Reading Center was set up at Belle Haven School using *Phonics Pathways*, resulting in significant improvement of reading scores. There are now over fifty dedicated tutors, and Stanford University has donated a portable building and various furnishings to house this program. The teaching materials and dedicated volunteers are rendering rave results from teachers and parents!" —Mary Shaw, Board Member
YES Reading Project
Menlo Park, CA

"*Phonics Pathways* has helped me immensely as an Orton-Gillingham tutor. It is both logically presented and easy to consult. Perhaps most importantly for dyslexic students, the pages of your book do not tend to strain students' eyes as do a number of other phonics books due to print size, style, or overcrowding. Students smile at 'Dewey the Bookworm' and his positive comments as they progress through your exercises. I will do my best to wear this book out, as well as share it with others who tutor."
—Roberta Puckett, Orton Tutor
Schofield, WI

"I am a Special Education Speech Technician, and have found *Phonics Pathways* to be a wonderful resource to use for reading and spelling lessons as well as with our Speech Therapy and ESL students. I like the fact that we can combine and reinforce so many programs through one easy-to-use publication. The word lists give many good examples of targeted sounds. The sample sentences are great for speech students who need to listen for correct pronunciations. We are still in the early stages of discovering all of its uses and applications, but I want to thank you for your excellent reading program."
—Danna Johnson, Speech Technician
Palisades School District, Palisades, WA

"I am currently serving as a volunteer tutor for adult literacy in the Salt Lake group, "Literacy Volunteers of America." For the past three months I have used *Phonics Pathways* in my classes. I have to tell you, the lessons you provide are marvelous and work very well with adults who are learning the basic reading skills. Thanks for your hard work in writing it—you have served more people than you know, and have made a major contribution to many people's lives!"
—Cynthia Skousen, Adult Literacy Volunteer
Salt Lake City, UT

"Our 3rd-grader's teacher told us he could not read. I got *Phonics Pathways* from the library, and in only four months Daniel was one of the best readers in his class! Also, he was just chosen 'student of the month.' As we worked with this book, I found I was also learning myself. This book should be obligatory reading for all first and second graders. Congratulations on writing a superb piece we so desperately need." —Richard M. Low, M.D.,
President, Infor*Med Medical Information Systems, Encino, CA

"After my mom had a stroke she had trouble getting words from her brain to her mouth. Soon after she was back home I began using *Phonics Pathways* with her—she loved it! The sounds were one of the problem areas she had, and it helped her so much. She is writing out her own Christmas cards and reading 'baby' books now. Today I'm proud to say that our library has its own copy of this book. We also have a growing population of Mexican families in our area, and I notice that many Hispanic children are using it to learn English."
—Barb Tessmann, Librarian
Oconomowoc Public Library, Oconomowoc, WI

"When parents ask us what they can do to help their children read, we always recommend *Phonics Pathways*. It is easy to use and engaging for children. We find that many children need to learn to track left to right with their eyes, and find patterns and similarities among words. These exercises provide that kind of practice. We use this book, and can heartily recommend it."
—Joanne Abey, Director
Tutorage Learning Center, Livermore, CA

"Our Ruth is hearing impaired, and has a cochlear implant which enables her to hear at about 30 decibels. Her ability to sound out words is limited, and until now she has made little progress in reading. The average reading level of deaf people in America is 4th grade, and we're deeply concerned about her reading. Your book now makes it easier, simpler, and more likely to succeed—we are systematically re-teaching all the phonics sounds. *Phonics Pathways* makes it a less anxious, more organized and 'do-able' task. We're with you in believing that even deaf students need a phonics base to break the barriers and become avid readers." —Mary Lou Powell
Las Cruces, NM

Other Books of Interest

Reading Pathways Simple Exercises to Improve Reading Fluency

5th Edition

Dolores G. Hiskes

Paper   ISBN: 978-0-7879-9289-7

http://www.josseybass.com

"With clarity, interest, humor, and precision, Dolores has offered a way out of the darkness of illiteracy. I am pleased to endorse [her] books as some of the finest instructional materials for teaching children and adults to read that I have reviewed." —**Robert W. Sweet Jr., professional staff member, Committee on Education and the Work Force, U.S. Congress, Washington, D.C.**

Reading Pathways will nurture and develop fluent reading skills in an effective and especially enjoyable fashion for grade level readers in K-3 and for struggling readers beyond. It aligns perfectly with *Phonics Pathways* but is an excellent adjunct to any other reading system.

This uniquely-formatted and progressive reading practice will help students:

- Acquire smooth blending skills
- Prevent or correct reversals
- Strengthen left-to-right eye tracking
- Improve and lengthen eye span

- Develop reading fluency
- Learn to syllabicate
- Ensure reading accuracy
- Increase vocabulary

Beginning with one word centered on top of the page, letters are blended into words and slowly-built into phrases and sentences of gradually increasing complexity. Every subsequent line is identical but has a few added words and is also centered, giving it the shape of a pyramid.

Short words then build by syllables into multisyllable words in mini-pyramids. Progressively more complex multisyllable word pyramids follow. Reading long words by syllables prevents guessing, ensures accuracy, and removes the fear and mystique of multisyllable words.

Dolores G. Hiskes has tutored reading for over thirty years. She lives in the Bay Area, where she has set up school and community tutoring programs and continues to write educational material, which can be seen at http://www.dorbooks.com. She can be reached at (925) 449-6983.

Other Books of Interest

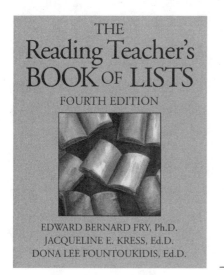

The Reading Teacher's Book Of Lists Fourth Edition

Edward B. Fry, Ph.D., Jacqueline Kress, Ed.D., Dona Lee Fountoukidis, Ed.D

Paper   ISBN: 0-13-028185-9

www.josseybass.com

Newly revised and updated, *The Reading Teacher's Book of Lists* puts at your fingertips over 190 of the most used and useful lists for developing instructional materials and planning lessons for elementary and secondary students.

Organized into fifteen sections for quick access—from Phonics, Useful Word and Vocabulary through Comprehension, Assessment and References—each brims with examples, key words, teaching ideas and activities you can use as is or easily adapt to meet your students' needs.

Moreover, all of the lists are printed in a convenient "lay-flat binding" for easy photocopying, to be used for individual students, small groups, or with the whole class.

A sampling of new lists found in the Fourth Edition:

- Suggested Phonics Teaching Order
- Books for Developing and Reluctant Readers
- Multiple Intelligences and Reading
- Comprehension Strategies
- Anagrams
- Speech Pronunciation

- 50 Reading Tips for Parents
- Rubrics for Writing
- Ways to Define a Word
- Internet Search Engines for Educators
- Web Sites for Reading, Writing & Literature

Edward B. Fry, Ph.D., is a Professor Emeritus of Education at Rutgers University (New Brunswick, NJ). At Rutgers, Dr. Fry was the director of the Reading Center and taught graduate and undergraduate courses in reading, curriculum, and other educational subjects. He lives in Laguna Beach, CA.

Jacqueline Kress, Ed.D., is Associate Dean and Director of Graduate Studies at Fordham University's Graduate School of Education (NY, NY) and works with the faculty in the preparation and professional development of educators. She lives in Elizabeth, NJ.

Dona Lee Fountoukidis, Ed.D., is director of Planning, Research, and Evaluation at William Paterson University (Wayne, NJ), where she conducts research on student learning. She lives in Kinnelon, NJ.